Nonproliferation and Threat Reduction Assistance: U.S. Programs in the Former Soviet Union

Amy F. Woolf
Specialist in Nuclear Weapons Policy

March 6, 2012

Congressional Research Service
7-5700
www.crs.gov
RL31957

CRS Report for Congress ————————————————
Prepared for Members and Committees of Congress

Summary

Congress passed the Nunn-Lugar amendment, authorizing U.S. threat reduction assistance to the former Soviet Union, in November 1991, after a failed coup in Moscow and the disintegration of the Soviet Union raised concerns about the safety and security of Soviet nuclear weapons. The annual program has grown from $400 million in the DOD budget to over $1 billion per year across three agencies—DOD, DOE, and the State Department. It has also evolved from an emergency response to impending chaos in the Soviet Union, to a more comprehensive threat reduction and nonproliferation effort, to a broader program seeking to keep nuclear, chemical, and biological weapons from leaking out of the former Soviet Union and into the hands of rogue nations or terrorist groups, to a global program to address the threat of weapons of mass destruction.

The Department of Defense manages the Cooperative Threat Reduction (CTR) Program, which provides Russia, Ukraine, Belarus, and Kazakhstan with assistance in transporting, storing, and dismantling nuclear, chemical, and biological weapons. U.S. assistance has helped these nations eliminate the delivery systems for nuclear weapons under the START Treaty, secure weapons storage areas, construct a storage facility for nuclear materials removed from weapons, construct a destruction facility for chemical weapons, and secure biological weapons materials.

The State Department manages the International Science and Technology Centers in Moscow and Kiev. These centers have provided research grants to scientists and engineers so that they will not sell their knowledge to other nations or terrorist groups. The State Department has also provided assistance with export and border control programs in the former Soviet states. The Department of Energy manages programs that seek to improve the security of nuclear warheads in storage and nuclear materials at civilian, naval, and nuclear weapons complex facilities. It also funds programs that help nuclear scientists and engineers find employment in commercial enterprises. DOE is also helping Russia dispose of plutonium removed from nuclear weapons and shut down its remaining plutonium-producing reactors by replacing them with fossil-fuel plants.

Analysts have debated numerous issues related to U.S. nonproliferation and threat reduction assistance. These include questions about the coordination of and priority given to these programs in the U.S. government, questions about Russia's willingness to provide the United States with access to its weapons facilities, questions about the President's ability to waive certification requirements so that the programs can go forward, and questions about the need to expand the efforts into a global program that receives funding from numerous nations and possibly extends assistance to others outside the former Soviet Union.

This report will be updated as needed.

Contents

Tables

Contacts

Introduction

In its FY2013 budget request, the Obama Administration is seeking around $880 million for threat reduction and nonproliferation programs in Russia and the other states of the former Soviet Union. This includes $519.1 million for DOD's Cooperative Threat Reduction Program, around $291.4 million for nonproliferation programs in the former Soviet Union, and about $70 million in funding for State Department programs. This total does not include funds for nonproliferation programs, such as the Global Threat Reduction Initiative (GTRI), Megaports, and the Nonproliferation and Disarmament Fund, which do not provide assistance within the former Soviet states.

Congress authorized around $1 billion for U.S. programs that provide nonproliferation and threat reduction assistance to Russia and the other states of the former Soviet Union in the FY2012 budget—including $508.2 million for DOD's Cooperative Threat Reduction (CTR) program, around $450 million for the Department of Energy's (DOE) nonproliferation programs in Russia, and around $75 million for State Department nonproliferation programs in the former Soviet Union.[1] With these programs, the United States seeks to help the recipient nations transport, store, and eliminate nuclear, chemical, and other weapons; secure and eliminate the materials used in nuclear, chemical, and biological weapons; and prevent proliferation of the knowledge needed to produce these weapons to nations or groups outside the former Soviet Union. Since FY1992, the United States has appropriated over $13 billion across these three agencies for these programs.[2]

During his tenure, President George W. Bush often voiced support for these programs. In November 2001, the White House noted that "The United States is committed to strong, effective cooperation with Russia and the other states emerging from the former Soviet Union to reduce weapons of mass destruction and prevent the proliferation of these weapons or the material and expertise to develop them."[3] At the U.S.-Russian summit in May 2002, the United States and Russia pledged to "continue cooperative threat reduction programs and expand efforts to reduce weapons-usable fissile material."[4] Furthermore, in June 2002, the President joined with the leaders of the G-8 nations to create the G-8 Global Partnership Against the Spread of Weapons and Materials of Mass Destruction. As is discussed in more detail later in this report, under this partnership, the United States committed to provide up to $10 billion over 10 years to pursue nonproliferation and threat reduction programs in Russia and the other former Soviet states.

President Obama has also embraced the goals of these programs, and has pledged to accelerate them. He pledged to "lead a global effort to secure all nuclear weapons materials at vulnerable sites within four years" and convened a summit of world leaders in Washington in April 2010 to

---

[1] The DOE budget request for nonproliferation assistance programs totaled more than $800 million and the State Department budget in these areas totaled around $125 million, but both include funding for programs outside the former Soviet Union.

[2] The term "spent" in this statement refers to the amount of money appropriated for threat reduction and nonproliferation programs. The amount of money actually paid to contractors for the work covered by these programs is less than the appropriated amount because many projects take years to complete, and payments may occur years after the money is appropriated.

[3] The White House. Office of the Press Secretary Fact Sheet. U.S. Government Nonproliferation and Threat Reduction Assistance to the Russian Federation. November 13, 2001.

[4] The White House. Office of the Press Secretary. Text of Joint Declaration. May 24, 2002.

address the international nuclear security agenda.[5] He appointed a "White House Coordinator for Nuclear Security" who, as a deputy national security advisor, coordinates U.S. threat reduction and nonproliferation programs.[6] In addition, President Obama and Russia's President Medvedev signed a Joint Statement on nuclear cooperation, in July, 2009, where they confirmed "their commitment to strengthening their cooperation to prevent the proliferation of nuclear weapons." The statement highlighted their continuing commitment to pursue a wide array of threat reduction and nonproliferation programs, to secure both their own nuclear materials and vulnerable nuclear materials around the world.[7] Moreover, in the 2010 Quadrennial Defense Review, released on February 1, 2010, the Department of Defense notes that it will expand its capabilities to counter weapons of mass destruction and support cooperative threat reduction efforts.[8]

Congress has also supported U.S. nonproliferation and threat reduction programs in the former Soviet states. Although some Members have questioned the value and effectiveness of some specific projects, Congress has authorized most of the funds requested by the executive branch in the 20 years since these programs began. Congress has also helped shape the programs, prohibiting funding for some types of projects and providing added funding for others.

Many analysts have questioned, however, whether the United States has done all that it could to prevent the leakage of knowledge, weapons, and materials from the former Soviet states. In its first budget submission in early 2001, the Bush Administration reduced funding for the DOD threat reduction programs by nearly 10% and cut more than $100 million out of DOE's defense nuclear nonproliferation programs, a funding category that includes U.S. nonproliferation assistance to Russia.[9] The Administration increased funding for these programs in FY2003, FY2004, and FY2006, but its budget for FY2005 and FY2007 for the DOD threat reduction programs again showed a 10% decrease. Even with increases in DOE budgets, some analysts argue that, when combined with declines in the DOD budget, the funding falls short of what is needed to address the continuing dangers of proliferation from the former Soviet states. Further, funding has begun to shift funding away from programs that secure weapons and materials in the former Soviet states and into programs that provide border security and assistance to a greater number of nations around the world. Some analysts support this shift in focus, and the emergence of a more global nonproliferation and threat reduction effort while others argue that this shift, if not accompanied by an increase in total funding, could undermine U.S. efforts to accelerate and complete programs with the former Soviet states. These concerns were evident in the congressional action on the FY2008 and FY2009 budgets, which increased several of the threat reduction and nonproliferation programs.

The current political environment may offer new challenges for these programs. Congress did not pass appropriations bills for FY2011, and, instead, provided funding through a continuing resolution (P.L. 112-10). With much of the FY2011 funding based on FY2010 budget levels,

---

[5] For more information on the goals of this summit and progress in securing vulnerable nuclear materials, see CRS Report R41169, *Securing Nuclear Materials: The 2010 Summit and Issues for Congress*, by Mary Beth Nikitin.

[6] See the White House website, The Agenda: Homeland Security. http://www.whitehouse.gov/agenda/homeland_security/

[7] The White House, Office of the Press Secretary, *Joint Statement by President Barack Obama of the United States of America and President Dmitry Medvedev of the Russian Federation on Nuclear Cooperation*, Moscow, July 6, 2009.

[8] U.S. Department of Defense, *Quadrennial Defense Review Report*, Washington, D.C., February 1, 2010, p. 35.

[9] Congress eventually restored the funding for DOE's Defense Nuclear Nonproliferation programs and added $223 million more in the FY2002 Emergency Supplemental Appropriations (P.L. 107-206) passed after the September 11, 2001 attacks.

some programs received more money than was requested in the FY2011 budget and others received significantly less funding. Moreover, some in Congress sought to fund the remainder of FY2011 at the levels provided in the FY2008 budget. This would have left U.S. threat reduction and nonproliferation assistance with funding that fell far short of the amounts requested, and according to some analysts, would have seriously undermined U.S. efforts to secure vulnerable nuclear materials and reduce the threat of nuclear terrorism.[10] Congress did not approve these deep cuts, however, and the funding for FY2011, although lower than the President's budget request, will sustain many of the ongoing efforts.

Many studies have offered recommendations for the size, shape, and operation of these programs that differ from the approaches taken by past Administrations. This report summarizes some issues raised in these reports and in congressional debates on the future of U.S. nonproliferation and threat reduction assistance. However, it first reviews the history of these programs, describing their origins in 1991, their expansion and evolution during the 1990s, and the changes in their direction during the first two years of the Bush Administration. The report also provides a broad summary of many of the program areas and projects supported by U.S. funding.

This report focuses on funding for threat reduction and nonproliferation programs in the states of the former Soviet Union. Although the United States has expanded its efforts to programs that seek to assist other nations in securing nuclear, biological, and chemical weapons materials, the overwhelming majority of U.S. funds still support programs in the former Soviet states. Nevertheless, because U.S. funding and focus has shifted in recent years, this report provides only a partial view of U.S. nonproliferation and threat reduction programs.

Background

The Nunn-Lugar Amendment

Congress initiated U.S. threat reduction and nonproliferation assistance to the Soviet Union in November 1991. A failed coup in Moscow in August 1991 and the subsequent disintegration of the Soviet Union had raised concerns about the safety and security of Soviet nuclear weapons. Consequently, Senators Nunn and Lugar proposed an amendment to the implementing legislation for the Conventional Armed Forces in Europe (CFE) Treaty (P.L. 102-228). The Senate passed the legislation by a vote of 86-8; the House adopted it through the conference report. This amendment, titled the "Soviet Nuclear Threat Reduction Act of 1991," authorized the use of $400 million in FY1992 Defense Department (DOD) funds to assist the Soviet Union, and its "successor entities" with efforts to "1) destroy nuclear weapons, chemical weapons, and other weapons, 2) transport, store, disable, and safeguard weapons in connection with their destruction; and 3) establish verifiable safeguards against the proliferation of such weapons."[11]

Senators arguing in support of the program, including Senators Nunn, Lugar, and Biden, emphasized the potential risks inherent in the Soviet collapse. They noted that the disintegration

---

[10] Michelle Marchesano and Kenneth Luango, *Funding Analysis of FY11 International WMD Programs*, Partnership for Global Security, Washington, D.C., January 2011, http://www.partnershipforglobalsecurity.org/PDFFrameset.asp? PDF=fy11_wmd_security_programs.pdf.

[11] For more information on this legislation, see CRS Report 94-985, *The Nunn-Lugar Program for Soviet Weapons Dismantlement: Background and Implementation*, by Theodor Galdi. (Available from Amy F. Woolf, on request.)

of the Soviet Union created "the danger that the ultimate disposition of nuclear weapons in the new political system will not be conducive to their safety or international stability," particularly if the weapons remained in several of the former Soviet republics. These Senators also warned of "a danger of seizure, theft, sale or use of nuclear weapons or components ... particularly if a widespread disintegration in the custodial system should occur." And third, they argued that "any weakening of control over weapons and components could spill outside the territory of the former Soviet Union, fueling nuclear proliferation worldwide."[12] Senator Nunn further warned that "we are on the verge of either having the greatest destruction of nuclear weapons in the history of the world or the greatest proliferation of nuclear weapons, nuclear materials, and scientific know-how on how to make these weapons, as well as chemical weapons, ballistic missiles, even biological weapons the world has ever seen."[13]

Senators who supported this legislation also emphasized that, by targeting "U.S. defense resources at the prompt, safe dismantlement of nuclear and chemical weapons in the Soviet arsenal,"[14] this assistance would "embody a new approach to enhancing our national security, an approach which fits a dramatically new national security environment."[15] Senator Biden further stated that, through this legislation, the United States would be "assisting ourselves," not the Soviet Union. But others questioned this characterization. They viewed the proposed assistance to the Soviet Union as foreign aid, which they opposed, and argued that the United States should instead use its defense resources to fund its own military and national security needs. Furthermore, some argued that, in providing assistance to the Soviet Union, the United States would allow the Soviet Union to divert its own resources away from the protection and dismantlement of its older weapons and towards the development and production of new weapons that could create new threats to the United States.[16] Members have raised these themes on numerous occasions over the years, debating whether U.S. nonproliferation and threat reduction assistance is a foreign aid program that provides benefits primarily to the recipients or a security program that provides benefits to both the United States and the former states of the Soviet Union.

Initially, Congress used the DOD budget to fund U.S. threat reduction assistance to the former Soviet States. In 1993, DOD began to refer to this effort as the Cooperative Threat Reduction (CTR) Program. Experts from other agencies, such as the State Department and Department of Energy, participated in the projects when their expertise was required. In FY1997 these agencies each took budgetary and management responsibility for the projects that relied on their expertise. Consequently, although many analysts and observers still use the title "Cooperative Threat Reduction Program" when referring to the full range of U.S. nonproliferation programs, this is no longer accurate. This report only uses the term "CTR" when referring to the threat reduction programs funded by the Department of Defense. It uses the phrase "threat reduction and nonproliferation assistance" to refer to the full range of programs in DOD, DOE, and State.

---

[12] See the comments of Senator Richard Lugar in the Congressional Record, November 25, 1991. p. S18005.

[13] Ibid. p. S18004.

[14] Senator Joe Biden, Congressional Record, November 25, 1991. p. S18002.

[15] Senator Sam Nunn, Congressional Record, November 25, 1991. p. S18004.

[16] See the comments of Senator Malcolm Wallop. Congressional Record, November 25, 1991. p. S18008.

A Slow Start

When Congress created the CTR program, many Members and experts outside government seemed to envision a relatively simple program where officials from the United States would travel to the four former Soviet states with nuclear weapons on their territories—Russia, Ukraine, Belarus, and Kazakhstan—to quickly safeguard and help dismantle nuclear, chemical, and other weapons. But the program's implementation was far slower and more complex than many expected. First, the need to develop and implement coordinated policies among several U.S. government agencies (primarily DOD, DOE, and the State Department) and within several organizations in the Pentagon slowed program implementation. Furthermore, the United States had to negotiate "umbrella agreements" with each recipient nation—setting out the privileges and immunities of U.S. personnel and to establishing the legal and customs framework for the provision of aid—before it could spend any money in the former Soviet states. Lingering mistrust between the parties, along with the high level of secrecy surrounding Russia's nuclear and chemical weapons programs complicated this process in 1992 and 1993.

During its first few years in office, the Clinton Administration sought to resolve the bureaucratic issues that had delayed the program. It offered broader political support to a cooperative relationship with Russia through a high level commission chaired by Vice President Gore and Russia's Prime Minister Chernomyrdin. This commission identified many efforts that later received funding through the CTR program. The Clinton Administration also provided significant policy and financial support to the CTR program, overcoming the reticence that had been expressed by some officials in the first Bush Administration. Consequently, it succeeded in sharply increasing the rate of expenditures on CTR projects by the mid-1990s. With the Administration's support, and with continuing congressional interest in the program, U.S. threat reduction and nonproliferation assistance began to expand and evolve. It expanded to several agencies, with DOE and the State Department each funding nonproliferation efforts in the former Soviet Union. It also expanded to include a broader range of programs. Where it had first focused on improving transportation security and helping with the destruction of strategic offensive nuclear weapons, it grew to include a wide range of efforts to secure and destroy nuclear, chemical, and biological weapons, the materials used in these weapons and the knowledge needed to design and produce these weapons. It has also expanded financially, from an initial level of approximately $400 million per year to a total of nearly $1 billion per year across the three agencies.

An Evolving Program

Initially, many in Congress saw U.S. assistance under Nunn-Lugar as an emergency response to impending chaos in the Soviet Union. Even after the sense of immediate crisis passed in 1992 and 1993, many analysts and Members of Congress remained concerned about the potential for diversion or a loss of control of nuclear and other weapons. Russia's economy was extremely weak and press accounts reported that nuclear materials from Russia were appearing on the black market in Western Europe. Consequently, many began to view CTR as a part of a long-term threat reduction and nonproliferation effort. Former Secretary of Defense William Perry referred to CTR as "defense by other means"[17] as the program helped eliminate Soviet weapons that had

---

[17] See, for example, U.S. Department of Defense. Cooperative Threat Reduction. April 1995. Washington, DC, p. 1.

threatened the United States and contain weapons and materials that could pose new threats in the hands of other nations.

By the mid-1990s, many observers also began to view U.S. assistance to the former Soviet states as a part of the effort to keep weapons of mass destruction away from terrorists. In 1996, experts testified to Congress that Russian nuclear and chemical facilities, with their crumbling security and lack of accounting procedures, could provide a source for terrorists seeking nuclear or chemical materials. In response, Congress expanded the programs that provided security at facilities with nuclear materials and suggested that more attention be paid to security at facilities with materials that could be used in chemical or biological weapons.[18] In January 2001, a task force sponsored by the Department of Energy stated that "the most urgent unmet national security threat to the United States today is the danger that weapons of mass destruction or weapons-usable materials in Russia could be stolen and sold to terrorists or hostile nation states and used against American troops abroad or citizens at home."[19] Since September 11, 2001, virtually all analysts who follow U.S. threat reduction and nonproliferation assistance have made the link between the possible quest for weapons of mass destruction by terrorists and the potential for thwarting them by helping Russia protect its weapons, materials, and knowledge.[20]

The Bush Administration also linked U.S. threat reduction and nonproliferation assistance to the former Soviet States to U.S. efforts to keep weapons of mass destruction away from terrorists. In early 2003, it stated that it had "expanded the strategic focus of the CTR program" to support the war on terrorism.[21] In its budgets presented between FY2004 and FY2007, it increased funding for several export and border control programs, for programs designed to stem the leakage of knowledge out of the former Soviet Union, and for an effort to find and recover "radiological sources"—a type of military device that could provide terrorists with nuclear materials for use in a "dirty bomb."[22] All of these initiatives focus more on stemming proliferation than on eliminating nuclear weapons in the former Soviet states. But it did not completely lose the initial focus. In February 2005, at the Bratislava summit, Presidents Bush and Putin agreed to accelerate some of the efforts to secure Soviet-era nuclear weapons. As is noted below, this agreement has shifted additional funding into some of the DOD CTR projects.

The Obama Administration has also emphasized that these programs, when implemented around the world, can help contain proliferation and reduce the threat of WMD terrorism. In testimony before the House Armed Services Committee, Dr. Michael Nacht, then the Assistant Secretary of Defense for Global Strategic Affairs, noted that the CTR program "is in a period of transition

---

[18] The March 1995 nerve agent attack in the Tokyo subway system by the Aum Shinryo cult raised the profile of this type of threat.

[19] The report went on to state that "unless protected from theft of diversion, the former Soviet arsenal of weapons of mass destruction threatens to become a goldmine for would-be proliferators the world over." Baker, Howard and Lloyd Cutler, Co-Chairs, Russia Task Force. A Report Card on the Department of Energy's Nonproliferation Programs with Russia. The Secretary of Energy Advisory Board, United States Department of Energy. January 10, 2001. p. 1.

[20] Senator Sam Nunn has stated that "Preventing the spread and use of nuclear biological, and chemical weapons and materials should be the central organizing principle on security for the 21st century." Remarks by Former U.S. Senator Sam Nunn, Chairman, Nuclear Threat Initiative. Carnegie Endowment for International Peace. International Nonproliferation Conference. November 14, 2002.

[21] U.S. Department of Defense. Fiscal Year 2004/2005 Biennial Budget Estimates. Former Soviet Union Threat Reduction Appropriation. February 2003. p. 1.

[22] Many analysts believe that this type of weapon, which could disperse radioactive materials across a wide area, might be particularly attractive to terrorists. For details see CRS Report RS21528, *Terrorist "Dirty Bombs": A Brief Primer*, by Jonathan Medalia.

from a nuclear-centric effort focused on the former Soviet Union to a more expansive effort to counter WMD threats throughout the world."[23] Funding requests over the past few years have demonstrated this shift, as the Obama Administration has moved beyond the program's historical base in the former Soviet Union and increased support for programs that seek to secure vulnerable materials around the world. Moreover, the Obama Administration has emphasized that, instead of providing assistance to nations in their efforts to contain their weapons of mass destruction, the program now focuses on efforts to engage other nations and foster cooperation between the United States and these nations in joint efforts to contain dangerous weapons and materials. While many of the projects may appear similar, the emphasis now is on efforts to form partnerships with other nations and to help them build their own capacity to stem secure and eliminate these materials.

Department of Defense Cooperative Threat Reduction Program

Program Objectives

At its inception, the CTR program sought to provide Russia, Ukraine, Belarus, and Kazakhstan with assistance in the safe and secure transportation, storage, and dismantlement of nuclear weapons. During the first few years, the mandate for U.S. assistance expanded to include efforts to secure materials that might be used in nuclear or chemical weapons, to prevent the diversion of scientific expertise from the former Soviet Union, to expand military-to-military contacts between officers in the United States and the former Soviet Union, and to facilitate the demilitarization of defense industries.[24] In 1994, Congress also indicated that threat reduction funds could be used to assist in environmental restoration at former military sites and to provide housing for former military officers who had been demobilized as a result of the dismantling of strategic offensive weapons. The 104th Congress reversed this position, however, banning the use of CTR funds for environmental restoration or housing for military officers. It also denied additional funding for the Defense Enterprise Fund, which focused on demilitarizing former Soviet defense industries.

By the mid-1990s, Congress and the Clinton Administration had agreed on a mandate for the CTR program that focused on the "core" objectives of securing and dismantling nuclear and chemical weapons, along with protecting against the proliferation of knowledge and materials that might be used in the production of these weapons by other nations. The Clinton Administration outlined this mandate in four key objectives for the CTR program:

- Destroy nuclear, chemical, and other weapons of mass destruction;

- Transport, store, disable, and safeguard these weapons in connection with their destruction;

---

[23] U.S. Congress, House Committee on Armed Services, Hearing. Dr. Michael L. Nacht, Assistant Secretary of Defense for Global Strategic Affairs, Statement for the Record. 111th Cong., 1st sess., July 15, 2009.

[24] For a more detailed description of the changes in the legislative mandate for the CTR program, see CRS Report 97-1027, *Nunn-Lugar Cooperative Threat Reduction Programs: Issues for Congress*, by Amy F. Woolf.

- Establish verifiable safeguards against the proliferation of these weapons, their components, and weapons-usable materials; and

- Prevent the diversion of scientific expertise that could contribute to weapons programs in other nations.[25]

In the late 1990s, Congress added funds to the CTR budget for biological weapons proliferation prevention; this effort has expanded substantially in recent years. Congress also expanded the CTR program to allow the use of CTR funds for emergency assistance to remove weapons of mass destruction or materials and equipment related to these weapons from any of the former Soviet republics, and from other nations around the world.

In its first budget, in FY2002, the Bush Administration reduced CTR funding by nearly 10% from over $440 million to $403 million. It also began a review of all U.S. threat reduction and nonproliferation assistance to Russia and the former Soviet states, stating that it sought to "ensure that existing U.S. cooperative nonproliferation programs with Russia are focused on priority threat reduction and nonproliferation goals, and are conducted as efficiently and as effectively as possible."[26] Some analysts welcomed the review, noting that it could provide an opportunity to revise and expand some programs, but others feared the review would lead to reductions in funding and the elimination of some programs.

When it announced the results of the review, the Bush Administration stated that it found that "most U.S. programs to assist Russia in threat reduction and nonproliferation work well, are focused on priority tasks, and are well managed."[27] But the review did signal a shift in the focus of U.S. nonproliferation and threat reduction assistance. Instead of highlighting projects aimed at the elimination of nuclear weapons, the Administration indicated that it would expand some projects that focused on chemical and biological weapons nonproliferation, including increasing funding for the construction of a controversial chemical weapons destruction facility in Russia. For many, this change seemed to be a natural response, in the post-September 11 environment, to growing concerns about the potential link between terrorism and weapons of mass destruction. Others, however, saw it as a retreat from the long-standing core objectives of the CTR program.

The Bush Administration confirmed this shift in focus with the release of its FY2004 budget request for CTR. Where it had requested and received $50 million in FY2002 and around $133 million in FY2003 for the construction of the chemical weapons destruction facility in Russia, it requested, and Congress authorized, $200.3 million in FY2004. This is nearly 45% of the total CTR budget request. The Bush Administration also increased funding for biological weapons proliferation prevention from $17 million in FY2002 to around $55 million in FY2003 and $54.2 million for FY2004. In contrast, funding for strategic offensive arms elimination in Russia declined from $133.4 million in FY2002 to $70.1 million in FY2003 and $57.6 million in FY2004.[28]

---

[25] U.S. Department of Defense. Cooperative Threat Reduction. April 1995. Washington, DC. p. 4.

[26] The White House. Fact Sheet. Administration Review of Nonproliferation and Threat Reduction Assistance to the Russian Federation. December 11, 2001.

[27] Ibid.

[28] The reduced request for FY2004 reflects, in part, the presence of unexpended balances from FY2003. The United States did not spend these funds because it could not initiate any new contracts during the period after the President did not certify Russia for participation in the CTR program and before Congress allowed the President to waive the certification requirement. See Statement of Dr. J.D. Crouch, II. March 4, 2003. p. 4.

Furthermore, in testimony before the House Armed Services Committee, J.D. Crouch, the Assistant Secretary of Defense for International Security Policy, stated that the Bush Administration had revised the four key objectives for CTR. The program would seek to:

- Dismantle FSU (former Soviet Union) WMD (weapons of mass destruction) and associated infrastructure;

- Consolidate and secure FSU WMD and related technology and materials;

- Increase transparency and encourage higher standards of conduct;

- Support defense and military cooperation with the objective of preventing proliferation.[29]

Although most ongoing CTR projects were consistent with these objectives, the absence of any specific reference to the destruction of nuclear weapons was notable. In addition, by stating that the United States seeks to "encourage higher standards of conduct," the Bush Administration indicated that it will place a higher priority on Russian openness, cooperation, and compliance with arms control agreements. This also presented something of a departure from the past, when the United States raised issues of transparency, openness, and compliance with Russia during private meetings, but did not tie these issues directly to the goals of the CTR program.

In its FY2010 Annual Report on the Cooperative Threat Reduction Program, DOD has offered a list of objectives for the CTR program that demonstrate further how the program has evolved to pursue broader nonproliferation and anti-terrorism objectives. The Report states that "CTR activities help deny rogue states and terrorists access to WMD and related materials, technologies, and expertise." It specifically notes that the program:

- dismantles strategic weapons delivery systems and infrastructure;

- enhances security and safety of WMD and fissile material during transportation and storage;

- consolidates and stores dangerous pathogens at risk for theft, diversion, accidental release, or use by terrorists;

- enhances partner states' capacities to develop early warning systems for bioterror attacks and potential pandemics;

- facilitates strategic research partnerships;

- helps prevent proliferation of WMD and related materials; and

- facilitates defense and military contacts to encourage military reform.[30]

---

[29] U.S. House. Committee on Armed Services Statement of Dr. J.D. Crouch II, Assistant Secretary of Defense for International Security Policy. March 4, 2003. p. 4. The Administration has formally incorporated these objectives into its planning for and reporting on the CTR Program. See U.S. Department of Defense. FY2006 CTR Annual Report to Congress. December 31, 2004. p. 1.

[30] U.S. Department of Defense, *Report on Activities and Assistance Under Cooperative Threat Reduction Programs*, FY2010 Annual Report, Washington, DC, July 7, 2009.

CTR Funding

When Congress first passed the Nunn-Lugar Amendment, it authorized the *transfer* of $400 million in FY1992 funds from other DOD accounts for threat reduction activities in the former Soviet Union. Few of these funds were spent in FY1992, so Congress extended the transfer authority for FY1992 funds and authorized the *transfer* of an additional $400 million from other DOD accounts in FY1993. In subsequent years, the Clinton Administration requested, and Congress authorized new appropriations for the CTR program. **Table 1** summarizes the amount of funding the Presidents requested for the CTR program and the amount authorized by Congress in each of the fiscal years between 1992 and 2006. Congress has authorized just under $9 billion for CTR since 1992.

Congress has approved the Administration's request for CTR funding in most years, but has added or reduced funding in some. In FY1996, the new Republican majority in the House questioned many elements of the CTR program and the House Armed Services Committee reduced funding to $200 million. The Senate had approved the Administration's request, and the conference committee agreed on a compromise of $300 million. The House also reduced the Administration's request in FY1997, approving $302.9 million for CTR, but the Senate *added* $37 million and the House eventually accepted the Senate's version in the conference committee.[31]

In FY2001, the House reduced President Clinton's request for CTR to $433 million. The Senate approved the full request and the conference committee settled on $443 million. This reduction was part of a dispute between the House, on one side, and the Senate and the Clinton Administration, on the other side, over funding for the chemical weapons destruction facility at Shchuch'ye in Russia. The House Armed Services Committee had reduced funding for that program in FY1998 and FY1999; in each of these two years, the Senate and the conference committee approved the Administration's requests. In FY2000, the House again eliminated all funding for the construction of Shchuch'ye and mandated, instead, that CTR fund security improvements at Russia's chemical weapons storage facilities. The conference committee accepted the House position, but still approved the Administration's request for $475.5 million for CTR. In FY2001, the Senate again accepted the House position banning funding for Shchuch'ye and, this time, accepted a small reduction in total funding for CTR.

In FY1996, when the Clinton Administration's request for CTR funding declined from $400 million to $371 million, total U.S. spending on threat reduction and nonproliferation assistance to Russia actually increased. In that year, the Materials Protection Control and Accounting Program (MPC&A) moved from DOD's CTR budget to the Department of Energy; the Clinton Administration requested and Congress authorized $70 million for DOE programs. In addition, $33 million in funding for the International Science and Technology Center in Moscow moved from the DOD budget to the State Department budget. In subsequent years, as is noted in more detail below, funding continued to grow for the DOE and State Department programs.

As is evident in the table below, the Bush Administration's request for CTR funding declined in both FY2007 and FY2008. For the most part, these declines reflected reductions in the funding

---

[31] This trend, with the House approving less than the President requested and the Senate approving the President's request, continued for several years. For details, see CRS Report 97-1027, *Nunn-Lugar Cooperative Threat Reduction Programs: Issues for Congress*, by Amy F. Woolf.

requested for the chemical weapons destruction facility at Shchuch'ye, as it neared completion, and, to a lesser extent, declines in funding for weapons elimination programs. The Administration did not propose to offset these reductions with increases in funding for new existing projects or the initiation of new projects. Congress did not accept this new funding profile in FY2008. Both chambers added funding for CTR programs. The House added $50 million, with $42.7 million going to the plant at Shchuch'ye and $7 million allocated to potential new initiatives in the CTR program. The Senate, for its part, added $80 million to the CTR budget request, with $50 million of this added funding going to biological weapons proliferation prevention. Funds were also added to the accounts for strategic offensive arms elimination in Russia and weapons of mass destruction proliferation prevention. The conference committee (H.Rept. 100-477, Title XIII) accepted the Senate's funding level, authorizing $428 million for CTR, with much of this added funding going to biological weapons proliferation prevention. The legislation also authorizes $10 million for new CTR initiatives that are outside the former Soviet Union. The conference committee did not retain the provision approved by the House that would fund new initiatives in CTR within the former Soviet Union. It did however, express support for such initiatives (H.Rept. 110-477, §1306) and request a study by the National Academy of Sciences that would assess possible initiatives and identify options for strengthening the program.

Congress also added funds to the Bush Administration's $414.1 million request for CTR for FY2009. The House authorized $445.1 million and the Senate authorized $434.1 million for these programs. The conference committee accepted that Senate funding level, adding $10 million $10.0 million for new initiatives, including activities in states outside of the former Soviet Union, $1.0 million for additional expenses associated with the Russian chemical weapons destruction activities, and an increase of $9.0 million for weapons of mass destruction proliferation prevention in the former Soviet Union.[32]

The Obama Administration, in its request for FY2010, sought $404.1 million for DOD's CTR program. This reduction again reflects the near-completion of many ongoing arms elimination projects, along with a decline in funding for biosecurity programs. As is noted below, however, the budget request does include increases for some CTR project areas, such as the Weapons of Mass Destruction Proliferation Prevention Program. Congress authorized $424.1 million for FY2010. The Administration has requested $522.5 million for CTR in FY2011. As is noted below, this added funding is allocated primarily to biosecurity programs and to a new initiative known as the Global Security Lockdown. Congress approved this request in the FY2011 Defense Authorization Act (P.L. 111-383) and in the final continuing appropriations act for FY2011. In FY2012, the Obama Administration requested $508.2 million for DOD's CTR program. Congress approved this request in the FY2012 Defense Authorization Act (P.L. 112-81). The Obama Administration has requested $519.1 million for this program in FY2013.

---

[32] P.L. 110-417, Title XIII.

Table 1. CTR Funding: Requests and Authorization

($ millions)

Fiscal Year	Request	Authorization
1992	$400	$400
1993	$400	$400
1994	$400	$400
1995	$400	$400
1996	$371	$300
1997	$328	$364.9
1998	$382.2	$382.2
1999	$440.4	$440.4
2000	$475.5	$475.5
2001	$458.4	$443.4
2002	$403	$403
2003	$416.7	$416.7
2004	$450.8	$450.8
2005	$409.2	$409.2
2006	$415.5	$415.5
2007	$372.3	$372.3
2008	$348.0	$428.05
2009	$414.1	$434.1
2010	$404.1	$424.1
2011	$522.5	522.5
2012	$508.2	$508.2
2013	$519.1	
Total FY1992-FY2010	$9239.009	$8790.85

CTR Projects

In its early years, the Department of Defense divided the CTR program into three distinct project areas—chain of custody, destruction and dismantlement, and demilitarization.[33] These distinctions faded over the years, as the program evolved and new projects entered the mix, although they provide a useful tool in reviewing the history of the program. In addition, in FY2012, the Obama Administration restructured the program and offered new categories for the different project

---

[33] This division, and the description in the next few paragraphs come from U.S. Department of Defense. Cooperative Threat Reduction. April 1995. Washington, DC. p. 5-6. The fourth category, "Other," includes administrative expenses and a special project on Arctic nuclear waste.

areas. Specifically, it combined several project areas that sought to improve security for nuclear weapons and materials into a single category known as "Global Nuclear Security."

Chain of Custody

Chain of custody activities were those designed to enhance safety, security, and control over nuclear weapons and fissile materials. Many of these were completed during the early years of CTR. These programs were created, in part, in response to early concerns about the safety and security of weapons and materials in transit. The United States and the recipient nations also found it easier to agree on the implementation of projects that focused on transit and storage of nuclear weapons and materials than to focus on destruction activities. The brief descriptions that follow summarize some of the key chain of custody activities.[34]

Transportation Security

When the Soviet Union collapsed, thousands of nuclear weapons were spread among four states (Russia, Ukraine, Belarus, and Kazakhstan), and, within each state, the weapons were dispersed among hundreds of deployment and storage areas. Soviet President Gorbachev and Russia's President Yeltsin had both committed to removing non-strategic nuclear weapons (those with ranges less than 3,600 miles) from non-Russian republics and storing them in a smaller number of facilities in Russia. In 1992, after signing the Lisbon Protocol to the START I Treaty, Ukraine, Belarus, and Kazakhstan also pledged to return all the warheads based on their territories to Russia.[35] **Table 2** summarizes the amount of money that the United States has appropriated for many of these transportation security projects through FY2011.

The United States has helped Russia improve the safety and security of nuclear weapons in transit. According to DOD, the CTR program "assists in the secure transport of 1,000-1,500 warheads per year." It has provided armored blankets to protect warheads in transit from potential attacks, storage containers to hold the warheads during transit, and assistance to enhance the safety and security of rail cars used to transport warheads from deployment to storage or dismantlement facilities. Ongoing transportation security projects also provide Russia with emergency response vehicles, training, and support equipment that it might need to respond to a nuclear weapons transportation accident. Funding for FY2005 supported the procurement and maintenance of specialized warhead transportation railcars.[36] The United States supported the movement of 45 train shipments in 2004. This number dropped to 24 shipments in 2005. The United States has required increased transparency for these shipments, and the process stopped between November 2004 and May 2005 while the United States and Russia resolved this issue. DOD is also helping Russia procure up to 100 new heated rail cars to replace aging existing rail cars as they are removed from service. DOD procured 19 of these rail cars through FY2009 and has begun production of another 23 cars. It has also verified the elimination of 38 older rail cars.

---

[34] The Defense Threat Reduction Agency http://www.dtra mil/oe/ctr/programs/index.cfm.

[35] For a description of the nuclear weapons based in non-Russian republics in 1991, see CRS Report RL32202, *Nuclear Weapons in Russia: Safety, Security, and Control Issues*, by Amy F. Woolf.

[36] Hoehn, William. *Preliminary Analysis of U.S. Department of Defense's Fiscal Year 2005 Cooperative Threat Reduction Budget Request*. RANSAC. February 10, 2004.

Congress authorized an additional $30 million for this project in FY2007; the Bush Administration requested, and both the House and Senate authorized, $37.7 million for FY2008. DOD initially indicated that it planned to support 70-72 shipments per year through 2011,[37] but it has reduced that number to no more than 4 shipments per month, or 48 per year, for FY2006, FY2007, and FY2008. It supported 45 rail shipments in FY2008.

Table 2. CTR Funding for Transportation Security

($ millions)

Project	Fiscal years	Total appropriation
Armored Blankets	FY1992-FY1993	$3.1
Emergency Response	FY1992-FY1996	$29.2
Railcar security enhancements	FY1992-FY1994	$21.5
Weapons Transportation Security	FY1995-FY2011	$355.4

Source: *Controlling Nuclear Warheads and Materials: A Report Card and Action Plan*, by Matthew Bunn, et al. Project on Managing the Atom. March 2003; Updated Funding Analysis of FY09 International WMD Security Programs, by Michelle Marchesano. Partnership for Global Security. July 2009.

DOD requested and Congress authorized $40.8 million for transportation security for FY2009. The Obama Administration requested, and Congress authorized, an additional 46.4 million for transportation security in FY2010. The Administration has requested $45 million for FY2011. According to DOD, this funding will support the transport of around 48 trainloads of deactivated nuclear warheads to storage or dismantlement sites. Congress authorized $45 million for this program in FY2011. The Obama Administration did not request any additional funding for this distinct program in FY2012, and instead, included it in the new Global Nuclear Security program area.

Weapons Storage Security

Several CTR projects have helped Russia improve security at storage facilities for strategic and tactical nuclear warheads. Russia has three types of storage sites—operational sites, storage sites, and rail transfer points. The United States does not provide assistance at operational sites. The Department of Energy has addressed security needs at rail transfer points that store warheads from the Russian Navy, and plans to do the same at one or more sites for the Strategic Rocket forces. Under the CTR program, DOD has enhanced security at both large "national stockpile storage sites" and smaller storage sites at Navy, Air Force, and Strategic Rocket Force bases.[38] DOD provided perimeter fencing, as a "quick fix" for vulnerable sites, and more comprehensive upgrades, including alarm systems and inventory control and management equipment to keep track of warheads in storage.

According to the GAO, this effort was slowed by Russia's reluctance to provide the United States with information about the precise number of sites in need of security upgrades and its refusal to

---

[37] U.S. Department of Defense. FY2006 CTR Annual Report to Congress. December 31, 2004. p. 43.

[38] The total number of sites remains classified. For details on DOD's plans, see U.S. General Accounting Office. *Weapons of Mass Destruction: Additional Russian Cooperation Needed to Facilitate U.S. Efforts to Improve Security at Russian Sites*. GAO-02-482. March 2003. p. 34.

allow the United States access to sites to design appropriate upgrades. For example, DOD purchased 123 kilometers of perimeter fencing for weapons storage sites; the Russian Ministry of Defense (MOD) said it would install the fences itself, but it has reportedly made little progress in doing so.[39] Furthermore, the United States purchased and tested equipment for comprehensive upgrades, but could not install it because Russia's MOD had not allowed the United States access to the interior of any storage facilities. The United States and Russia completed agreements in February 2003 that have provided the United States with a degree of access to these sites.[40] U.S. personnel can now conduct site assessments and other activities that support the installation of physical security upgrades at a number of weapons storage locations. This change is reflected in significant increases in funding for site security enhancements in the FY2005 and FY2006 budget requests for CTR. The United States has plans to provide security enhancements at up to 42 permanent storage sites and temporary handling sites in Russia.[41] In 2005, during the Bratislava summit, Presidents Bush and Putin pledged to accelerate work on weapons storage security, and, as a result, both DOD and DOE report that they had completed their work of installing security upgrades by the end of 2008. In a complementary effort, the United States has constructed a Security Assessment and Training Center so that DOD and MOD personnel can test and select security systems for weapons storage sites. The United States is also helping Russia develop training programs for personnel with access to nuclear weapons.

Between FY1995 and FY2010, DOD appropriated around $831.8 million for weapons storage security.[42] The Bush Administration requested $74.1 million in FY2006, and reprogrammed $10 million intended for strategic offensive arms elimination to this program area in FY2006, leading to a total appropriation of $84.1 million. It also requested an additional $44.5 million in the FY2006 Emergency Supplemental Appropriations package for effort. Then, it requested an additional $87.1 million for FY2007. Congress approved the added funding in the Emergency Supplemental Bill and authorized 74.1 million for FY2007. The Administration requested only $23 million for warhead storage security for FY2008; Congress increased this amount to $47.64 million in the conference report on the FY2008 Defense Authorization Bill.

The increases in funding for warhead security through FY2007 reflect the commitment made by Presidents Bush and Putin in February 2005 to accelerate the warhead security upgrades. After Russia identified all the sites in need of upgrades, the United States agreed to provide assistance at 15 sites, 8 with funding from the CTR program and 7 with funding from the DOE nonproliferation budget. Because they have completed these upgrades, they have begun to shift funding towards sustainment activities, rather than further upgrades. The FY2009 request for weapons storage security declined to $24.1 million, as a result of this shift to sustain and support the systems that have been installed in previous years. Congress approved this request for FY2009.

The Obama Administration requested, and Congress authorized, $15.1 million for weapons storage security in FY2010. The appropriation for FY2010, however, increased to $22.1 million. The budget for FY2011 includes a request for $9.6 million for this effort. Much of this funding

---

[39] Ibid. p. 36.

[40] U.S. House. Committee on Armed Services. Statement of Dr. J.D. Crouch, Assistant Secretary of Defense for International Security Policy. March 4, 2003.

[41] U.S. Department of Defense. FY2006 CTR Annual Report to Congress. December 31, 2004. p. 41.

[42] *Controlling Nuclear Warheads and Materials: A Report Card and Action Plan*, by Matthew Bunn, et al. Project on Managing the Atom. March 2003.

will be used to continue sustainment efforts at secure storage sites. Congress authorized this amount in the FY2011 Defense Authorization Act and the continuing resolution for FY2011.

In FY2012, the Administration requested funding for weapons storage security activities in the new Global Nuclear Security program area. It did not specify how much of the funding in this program area would go to weapons storage security.

Fissile Materials Storage

According to unclassified estimates, Russia inherited more than 30,000 nuclear warheads from the Soviet Union, along with enough plutonium and highly enriched uranium (HEU) to produce thousands more warheads. As it consolidates and reduces its arsenal, Russia has begun to dismantle thousands of these warheads. Several CTR projects seek to improve the long-term security of the fissile materials removed from these weapons. **Table 3** summarizes the amount of money that the United States appropriated for projects related to storage of fissile materials in Russia.

The United States provided Russia with more than 26,000 containers to hold the fissile materials; it also helped Russia design and build a highly secure storage facility at Mayak that will provide long-term safe and secure storage for these materials. This facility will hold the equivalent of fissile material from 25,000 nuclear warheads. The first wing of this building was completed and certified for use in December 2003; it is now ready to receive nuclear materials for storage.[43] The United States and Russia no longer plan to construct an expected second wing.[44] The United States and Russia are still working, with little progress, to complete a "transparency agreement" that will allow the United States to confirm that materials stored in the facility actually came from dismantled warheads. The State Department has pursued this agreement. Even without the completion of this agreement, however, the Mayak facility began to accept nuclear materials for storage in July 2006

Table 3. CTR Funding for Fissile Materials Storage

($ millions)

Project	Fiscal years	Total appropriation
Fissile Material Containers	FY1992-FY2000	$82.2
Storage Facility Design	FY1993	$15
Storage Facility Construction	FY1994-FY2001	$387

Source: *Controlling Nuclear Warheads and Materials: A Report Card and Action Plan*, by Matthew Bunn, et al. Project on Managing the Atom. March 2003.

---

[43] U.S. Senate. Committee on Armed Services. Cooperative Threat Reduction Program. Testimony of Lisa Bronson, Deputy Undersecretary of Defense for Technology Security Policy and Counterproliferation. March 10, 2004. (Herein after referred to as Bronson Testimony.)

[44] The absence of funding for the second wing of Mayak was responsible for a significant portion of the decline in the Bush Administration request for CTR funding, from $443 million in FY2001 to $403 million, in FY2002.

Destruction and Dismantlement

Destruction and dismantlement projects help with the elimination of nuclear, chemical, and other weapons and their delivery vehicles. These projects have helped Russia, Ukraine, Belarus, and Kazakhstan remove warheads, deactivate missiles, and eliminate launch facilities for the nuclear weapons covered by the START treaty. The Clinton Administration, and some analysts outside government, credited U.S. assistance in this area with providing Ukraine, Belarus, and Kazakhstan with an incentive to relinquish the nuclear weapons on their territories in the early 1990s.[45] When the Soviet Union collapsed in 1991, it had more than 11,000 warheads deployed on nearly 1,400 ICBMs, 940 SLBMs and 162 heavy bombers. According to the Defense Threat Reduction Agency, the CTR program has helped deactivate more than 7,500 warheads, 768 ICBMs, 651 SLBMs, and 155 heavy bombers.[46] More than half of the funds appropriated for CTR support projects in this category. Some of the key areas of destruction and dismantlement projects are described below.

Strategic Offensive Arms Elimination

The United States has provided Russia, Ukraine, Belarus, and Kazakhstan with assistance in eliminating the launchers and infrastructure associated with strategic nuclear weapons deployed on their territories. This effort is complete in Belarus and Kazakhstan; it continues in Russia, and, to a lesser extent, Ukraine. In each of these nations, the United States has provided the recipient nations with technology and expertise needed to deactivate and dismantle missiles, launchers, submarines, and bombers. According to the CTR Scorecard, the United States has, thus far, eliminated nearly 1,400 ballistic missiles and has deactivated over 7,500 warheads on former Soviet strategic nuclear forces.[47] It has also helped construct storage facilities for missiles removed from deployment and fuel removed from deactivated missiles.

The United States and Ukraine have been working on a method to eliminate rocket motors from SS-24 ICBMs. DOD did not request any more funding for this project area in FY2006 and planned to complete ongoing work with prior year funds, because the two nations could not agree on a method to eliminate these rocket motors. However, a low level of funding has resumed in recent years, as the United States now supports the safe storage of 160 rocket motors from SS-24 missiles and buys the casings from Ukraine after Ukraine has removed the propellant. Ukraine is financing, on its own, the construction and operation of a water washout facility for this purpose. The Bush Administration requested, and Congress authorized $6.4 million for the U.S. portion of this effort in FY2009. The Obama Administration requested, and Congress authorized, an additional $6.8 million for FY2010. The Obama Administration requested, and Congress authorized, an additional $6.8 million for this project in FY2011; this funding will continue to support the storage of SS-24 rocket motors, while Russia constructs the elimination facility for them.

In Russia, the United States is helping to eliminate and dismantle SS-18 and SS-19 ICBMs, disassemble and eliminate components of the SS-N-20 SLBM, eliminate SS-25 ICBMs and their road-mobile launchers, and destroying rail-mobile SS-24 ICBMs and their launchers. For

---

[45] U.S. Department of Defense. *Cooperative Threat Reduction.* April 1995. Washington, DC. p. 1.

[46] For the full CTR scorecard, see Defense Threat Reduction Agency, http://www.dtra mil/oe/ctr/scorecard.cfm.

[47] http://lugar.senate.gov/nunnlugar/scorecard html

FY2006, DOD requested $78.9 million for this project area, an increase of around $20 million over the budget in FY2005. The increase reflected the fact that Russia had added more missiles and launchers to the destruction schedule to meet the terms of the Moscow Treaty. However, after Congress appropriated the requested amount, the Administration reprogrammed funding out of this project area, leaving only $49.7 million. As was noted above, it transferred $10 million to weapons storage security. It also transferred $1.1 million to strategic offensive arms elimination programs in Ukraine and will lose around $5 million in recisions imposed by Congress. The Bush Administration requested $77 million for this project area in FY2007; Congress approved $78.9 million. It requested $77.9 million for FY2008. The House approved this amount; the Senate, however, increased funding for strategic offensive arms elimination in Russia to $102.9 million. According to the Senate Armed Service Committee Report on this legislation (S.Rept. 110-77), this increase of $25 million should be used to "accelerate the completion of activities at sites ... where the materials and weapons are stored" and to facilitate the consolidation, dismantlement, and disposition of these weapons and materials. The conference committee (H.Rept. 110-477) allocated $92.885 million to this project area. DOD requested $79.9 million for Strategic Offensive Arms Elimination in Russia, FY2009; Congress authorized these amounts.

The Obama Administration requested an additional $66.4 million in FY2010. Congress authorized this amount in the FY2010 Defense Authorization Act. The Administration requested, and Congress authorized, $66.7 million for this project area in FY2011. This funding supports efforts to assist Russia in eliminating SS-19 and SS-25 ICBMs and their launchers, and in completing the dismantlement of a Russian Typhoon submarine. It requested an additional $63.2 million for this project area in FY2012; this amount includes funding for both the strategic offensive arms elimination activities in Russia and those in Ukraine. Congress authorized this amount. According to the Administration, this funding will continue to support the elimination of SS-18 and SS-19 ICBM silo launchers, SS-25 ICBMs and their launchers, SS-N-18 SLBMs, and the reactor core and launcher section of one Delta-IV submarine. The Administration has requested $68.3 million for this project area in FY2013.

One project funded in this category, the construction of a plant to dispose of liquid fuel removed from Soviet ICBMs, raised concerns among some in Congress during the Bush Administration. The United States constructed the facility at a cost of nearly $100 million. However, during construction, Russia used much of the fuel in rockets in its space-launch program. Consequently, in 2002, Russia informed the United States that it did not have any fuel for the facility.[48] Representative Duncan Hunter stated that the episode represented an example of the potential for waste in the CTR program.[49] Others, however, note that, although unfortunate, this case is the exception in a program that has spent more than $4 billion on threat reduction projects.

Table 4 summarizes the amount of money that the United States has appropriated for several key strategic offensive arms elimination projects.[50]

---

[48] U.S. House. Committee on Armed Services. Statement of David K. Steensma, Deputy Assistant Inspector for Auditing, Department of Defense Office of the Inspector General. March 4, 2003.

[49] Hunter, Duncan. "Wasteful 'Threat Reduction' in Russia." *Washington Post*. March 4, 2003. p. 23.

[50] For a more detailed breakdown of projects in this program area, see U.S. House. Committee on Armed Services. Statement of Dr. J.D. Crouch, Assistant Secretary of Defense for International Security Policy. March 4, 2003. p. 4. See also U.S. Department of Defense. Fiscal Year 2004/2005 Biennial Budget Estimates. Former Soviet Union Threat Reduction Appropriation. February 2003. pp. 16-21.

Table 4. CTR Funding for Strategic Offensive Arms Elimination (SOAE)

($ millions)

Nation	Fiscal years	Total appropriation
Russia	FY1993-FY2012	$1745.9a
Ukraine	FY1993-FY2011	$590.8
Kazahkstan	FY1994-FY1996	$64.6
Belarus	FY1994-FY1996	$3.3

Source: *Controlling Nuclear Warheads and Materials: A Report Card and Action Plan*, by Matthew Bunn, et al. Project on Managing the Atom. March 2003.

a. Beginning in FY2012, the budget request combined funding for Russia and Ukraine; this combined funding is added to the total for Russia.

WMD Infrastructure Elimination

Through the CTR program, the United States has helped Ukraine eliminate equipment and facilities that supported the deployment and operation of nuclear weapons. These facilities include liquid missile propellant storage facilities, nuclear weapons storage facilities, and infrastructure at bomber bases. The United States also helped Kazakhstan secure fissile materials and eliminate facilities at a nuclear weapons storage area and a former chemical weapons production facility.[51] Between FY1994 and FY2003, DOD appropriated $38.2 million for this program in Ukraine and $44.5 million in Kazakhstan. It has not requested any additional funds in subsequent years.

Chemical Weapons Destruction

The Soviet Union had the largest stockpile of chemical weapons in the world. Russia declared this stockpile to contain 40,000 metric tons of chemical weapons. The United States has questioned the accuracy and completeness of this declaration, a factor that contributed to Russia's loss of certification for CTR programs in FY2002. Russia's chemical weapons are stored at seven sites in Russia; five sites contain nerve agents in bombs and artillery shells, and three of these sites and two additional sites house bulk stocks of blister agents.[52] Russia has committed, under the Chemical Weapons Convention (CWC), to destroy these stocks by 2007 (it has requested an extension until 2012), but it contends that it lacks the financial resources to meet this deadline. A European consortium, led by Germany, has constructed a destruction facility at Gorny to destroy the blister agent.[53] The United States is assisting Russia with the design and construction of a facility at Shchuch'ye to destroy all of Russia's nerve agent. The chemical weapons storage facility at Shchuch'ye contains nearly half of Russia's stockpile of artillery shells filled with

---

[51] U.S. Department of Defense. Fiscal Year 2004/2005 Biennial Budget Estimates. Former Soviet Union Threat Reduction Appropriation. February 2003. p. 9.

[52] U.S. General Accounting Office. *Weapons of Mass Destruction: Additional Russian Cooperation Needed to Facilitate U.S. Efforts to Improve Security at Russian Sites.* GAO-02-482. March 2003. pp. 58-59.

[53] For a description of this facility and program see Glasser, Susan B. "Cloud Over Russia's Poison Gas Disposal." *Washington Post.* August 24, 2002. p. 1

nerve agent.[54] The new facility is intended to destroy these stocks and those stored at the other four storage sites, an amount estimated to be around 5,450 metric tons.

Construction on this facility began in March 2003. The United States also helped install equipment at the destruction facility and to train the operating personnel. The United States and Russia had hoped that construction would be completed and the facility would begin operations by the end of 2008. It would then take around 3.5 years to destroy the stocks of nerve agent, allowing Russia to meet the 2012 deadline. Operations at the facility began in March 2009, and was officially dedicated in late May 2009.[55] As of September 2011, Russia had eliminated over 2,365 metric tons of nerve agent at Shchuch'ye.

This project has been at the center of much debate during the past ten years. In FY1999, the House tried to reduce the amount of CTR funding requested for Shchuch'ye by $53.4 million, arguing that Russia's chemical weapons posed more of an environmental problem for Russia than a threat to U.S. security.[56] The Defense Authorization Bills for FY2000 and FY2001 prohibited any additional funding for Shchuch'ye. Congress resumed funding Shchuch'ye in FY2002, when the Bush Administration requested $50 million for the project. However, in FY2003, when the Bush Administration requested $133.6 million for Shchuch'ye, the House balked again and approved $50 million. The House Armed Services Committee argued that the program could not absorb such a large increase in one year and, because Russia did not yet appear committed to the elimination of its chemical weapons, that the United States should not accelerate its efforts. The conference report (H.Rept. 107-772) also limited funding for Shchuch'ye to $50 million, but it stated that the Administration could use the remaining $83.6 for other projects related to the storage and elimination of nuclear weapons, or for chemical weapons destruction if Russia provides a "full and accurate" disclosure of its chemical weapons stockpile.

The Bush Administration requested $200 million for this project in FY2004. The Senate approved this amount, but the House, in its version of the FY2004 Defense Authorization Bill (H.R. 1588), reduced the funding to $171.5 million. It also mandated that the United States could only release funds in excess of $71 million if Russia and other nations contributed to the project. Specifically, the U.S. contribution could not exceed the other nations' contribution by more than a factor of two. These provisions reflect concerns expressed by some in the House about a lack of financial commitment from Russia and other European nations to the Shchuch'ye project. The conference committee rejected the House position, approving the full $200 million for Shchuch'ye and eliminating the linkage of U.S. funding to funding from other nations. Nevertheless, by December 2003, six other countries had contributed $69 million to the project.[57]

The Bush Administration requested, and Congress authorized, $158.4 million for Shchuch'ye in FY2005. The reduction in funding for this project represented most of the reduction in the overall CTR budget between FY2004 and FY2005. This reduction in funding did not derive from any significant policy debates about the project; instead, it occurred because the FY2004 budget

---

[54] The Department of Defense estimates this to be 5,460 metric tons of agent in nearly 2 million rocket and artillery warheads. See U.S. Department of Defense. Fiscal Year 2004/2005 Biennial Budget Estimates. Former Soviet Union Threat Reduction Appropriation. February 2003. p. 4

[55] Jim Heintz, "U.S, Russian Officials Open Plant to Destroy Chemical Weapons," *Boston Globe*, May 30, 2009. See, also, "New Russian Chemical Weapons Site Begins Operations," *Global Security Newswire*, March 6, 2009.

[56] U.S. Congress, House, Committee on National Security. National Defense Authorization Act For Fiscal Year 1999. Report 105-532, Washington, DC. May 12, 1998. p. 352.

[57] Bronson Testimony, March 10, 2004.

---

included funding for a one-time investment in capital-intensive construction equipment. The United States did not need to repeat this investment in FY2005.[58] The Administration requested, and received, an additional $108.5 million in its budget for FY2006. It requested only $42.7 million for this project in FY2007; Congress approved this request. The Bush Administration indicated that the reduction reflected the maturity of the project and the lack of any further capital investment.

The Bush Administration did not request any additional funding for the Shchuch'ye plant in the FY2008 budget. This lack of funding raised eyebrows among analysts outside government, as work at the facility was not yet complete and the facility was not yet operating. The House Armed Services Committee also questioned this approach and added nearly $43 million to the budget in the FY2008 Defense Authorization Bill for Shchcuch'ye. In its report on the bill (H.Rept. 110-477), the committee noted that it did not believe that DOD could complete the project without additional funding, as the existing budget did not account for the rising costs of construction materials in Russia. The conference committee approved $6 million for this project area, allowing some work to continue during FY2008. Congress also required that the Secretary of Defense submit a report on the strategy and cost estimates for completing the Shchcuch'ye project. The Administration again did not request any funding for Shchcuch'ye in FY2009; Congress added $1 million.

Congress also authorized $3 million for Shchcuch'ye in FY2010, and the Obama Administration requested, and Congress authorized, an additional $3 million for FY2011. Some analysts outside government believe the United States will have to provide more funding for this facility in the future. The Obama Administration requested, and Congress approved, $9.8 million for this effort in FY2012. The Administration requested an additional $14.6 million for this project area in FY2013. Some of this funding will allow the United States to provide technical support to Russia in its operation the Kizner CWDF destruction facility.

In the past, Congress has subjected funding for Shchuch'ye to a number of certifications. For example, it stated that the President must certify that Russia is committed to providing at least $25 million per year to help construct and operate the facility; that Russia was committed to destroying all its remaining nerve agent; that other nations were committed to contributing to the construction of this facility; and that Russia is forthcoming with data about its chemical weapons stockpile. The President requested that Congress allow him to waive the certification requirement, so that construction could continue, even if Russia has not met all the conditions. Congress provided the President with waiver authority, but only for one year, in the FY2003 Defense Authorization Bill (P.L. 107-248).[59] It extended this waiver authority by one more year in the FY2004 Defense Authorization Bill (H.R. 1588); the Administration submitted this waiver in early December 2003.[60] For FY2005, the Senate approved unlimited waiver authority for the President, but the House again limited this authority to one year. The House prevailed in conference, with an adjustment to allowing the waiver authority through the end of the calendar

---

[58] Ibid.

[59] The waiver authority for the certification requirements from Shchuch'ye is different from the waiver authority the President sought for the broader certification requirements included in the CTR legislation. These are discussed in more detail below.

[60] Memorandum for the Secretary of State, Presidential Determination No. 2004-10. Presidential Determination on Waiver of Conditions on Obligation and Expenditure of Funds for Planning, Design, and Construction of a Chemical Weapons Destruction Facility in Russia. The White House. December 9, 2003.

year, rather than the fiscal year (see P.L. 108-375). Congress extended this waiver authority through 2011.

Biological Threat Reduction

The Soviet Union reportedly developed the world's largest biological weapons program, employing an estimated 60,000 people at more than 50 sites. This weapons complex developed a broad range of biological pathogens for use against plants, animals, and humans.[61] Russia reportedly continued to pursue research and development of biological agents in the 1990s, even as the security systems and supporting infrastructure at its facilities began to deteriorate. The United State began to provide Russia with CTR assistance to improve safety and security at its biological weapons sites and to help employ biological weapons scientists during the late 1990s, even though Russia has not provided a complete inventory of the sites or people involved in biological weapons work.[62]

The CTR program has supported four separate BTR programs, working at dozens of sites that include many weapons facilities. Through the Biological Weapons Infrastructure Elimination program, the United States helped Russia eliminate the infrastructure and equipment at those Biological Research and Production Centers (BRPCs) that have the capability to produce biological weapons. Through the Biosecurity and Biosafety program, the United States is helping to enhance safety and security at these centers to ensure the safe and secure storage and handling of biological pathogens. This program has been combined with the BW Threat Agent Detection and Response program, which seeks to develop modern surveillance, warning, and response networks and to help secure Russia's central storage facilities for BW pathogens. Finally, through Cooperative Biodefense Research, the United States and Russia are using cooperative research projects to increase transparency and discourage the "leakage" of Russian biological weapons knowledge to other nations. Each of these programs is implemented through the International Science and Technology Centers, because DOD has been unable to conclude implementing agreements with the relevant ministries in Russia.[63]

The Biological Threat Reduction program also supports activities in other former Soviet states, including Azerbaijan, Georgia, Kazakhstan, Ukraine, and Uzbekistan. DOD is also negotiating an agreement to begin work in Armenia. For example, CTR funding helped destroy the huge biological weapons production facility in Stepnogorsk, Kazakhstan.

The potential proliferation of biological weapons poses one of the key challenges for U.S. nonproliferation assistance to Russia.[64] According to the General Accounting Office, progress in gaining Russia's cooperation and implementing these projects has been very slow. The United States has found it particularly difficult to gain access to four key military facilities. The problem

---

[61] For more details on the BWPP programs, see CRS Report RL31368, *Preventing Proliferation of Biological Weapons: U.S. Assistance to the Former Soviet States,* by Michelle Stem Cook and Amy F. Woolf.

[62] U.S. General Accounting Office. *Weapons of Mass Destruction: Additional Russian Cooperation Needed to Facilitate U.S. Efforts to Improve Security at Russian Sites.* GAO-02-482. March 2003. pp. 48-49.

[63] Ibid. p. 54.

[64] "The security of existing pathogen libraries, the past scope of work, the current whereabouts of BW and BW-related experts, and the future disposition of the FSU biological weapons capability are all critical concerns within the threat reduction agenda." *Reshaping U.S.-Russian Threat Reduction: New Approaches for the Second Decade. Carnegie Endowment for International Peace and Russian American Nuclear Security Advisory Council.* November 2002. p. 2.

is further aggravated by the fact that Russia is reducing the size of its complex, leaving many scientists potentially unemployed or underemployed. In addition, biological pathogens are small and easily transported, further increasing the proliferation risk.[65]

Between FY1997 and FY2011, DOD appropriated around $1.1 billion for these projects, with significant increases in the amount of both the request and the appropriation in recent years. The Bush Administration requested $54.2 million for these programs in FY2004. Congress approved this amount but attached some restrictions to the funding. In its version of the FY2004 Defense Authorization Bill (H.R. 1588), the House had sought to prohibit funding cooperative research at any site in the Soviet Union until the Secretary of Defense could certify that the site did not house any prohibited biological weapons research, until the facility had conducted an assessment of its vulnerability to the loss or theft of pathogens and until it had begun to implement measures to reduce its vulnerability to the loss or theft of biological agents. The conference committee modified this measure, stating that CTR could not fund cooperative research at a facility until the Secretary of Defense determines that no prohibited research occurs at the facility and until the facility plans to implement appropriate security measures. It also permitted the use of up to 25% of the funds authorized for the project to be expended on making these determinations.

The Bush Administration requested, and Congress authorized, a similar amount—$55 million— for biological weapons proliferation prevention in FY2005. However, within this total, the Administration shifted funding away from Cooperative Biodefense Research projects, reducing this area from $36.6 million in FY2004 to $13.1 million in FY2005, towards bio-security and bio-safety efforts. This shift reflected, in part, the congressional concerns with possible U.S. support for ongoing Russian biological weapons programs. It also derived from the Administration's plans to expand U.S. bio-safety and bio-security assistance into facilities in Kazakhstan and Uzbekistan and Georgia.[66] The Bush Administration requested, and Congress approved, an additional $60.8 million for BW proliferation prevention in FY2006. It requested an additional $68.4 million for FY2007, and the 109th Congress approved this request in the FY2007 Defense Authorization Bill. This legislation also mandated that the National Academy of Sciences pursue a study that would analyze the challenges and identify opportunities for further cooperation between Russian and the United States on biological weapons proliferation prevention.

The Bush Administration requested $144.5 million for Biological Weapons Threat Reduction programs in FY2008, with the funding split between Biosecurity, Biosafety, and Threat Agent Detection and Response ($125.75 million) and Cooperative Biological Research ($18.75 million). This request represents a significant expansion in U.S. biological weapons nonproliferation assistance for the Soviet Union and reflects growing concerns about the threat of biological weapons proliferation. But some believe this increase may not be sufficient. Senator Richard Lugar sought to add $100 million for the CTR program in FY2008, with the express purpose of expanding and accelerating biological weapons nonproliferation programs.[67] The Senate reduced this amount but still added $50 million to the program for FY2008. According to the Senate Armed Services Committee Report on the bill (S.Rept. 110-77), this funding would support

---

[65] U.S. General Accounting Office. *Weapons of Mass Destruction: Additional Russian Cooperation Needed to Facilitate U.S. Efforts to Improve Security at Russian Sites*. GAO-02-482. March 2003. pp. 44-46.

[66] Hoehn, William. *Preliminary Analysis of U.S. Department of Defense's Fiscal Year 2005 Cooperative Threat Reduction Budget Request*. RANSAC. February 10, 2004.

[67] Lugar Wants $100 Million Nunn-Lugar Budget Increase. Press Release. Office of Senator Richard Lugar. February 5, 2007.

programs throughout the former Soviet Union and accelerate high-priority efforts. The committee also requested that the National Academy of Sciences prepare a report on how the United States might cooperate with other nations in preventing the proliferation of biological weapons. The conference committee (H.Rept. 110-477) authorized $158.5 million for this program area and retained the request for a study by the National Academy of Sciences. The Bush Administration further increased the request for BWTR program in FY2009 to $184.5 million. As in FY2008, these funds were being split between Biosecurity, Biosafety, and Threat Agent Detection and Response ($160 million) and Cooperative Biological Research ($24.4 million). Congress authorized this request for FY2009.

The Obama Administration requested $152 million for Biological Threat Reduction in FY2010. Within this request, the Biosafety, Biosecurity, and Threat Agent Detection and Response program would receive $133.3 million, a reduction from its FY2009 appropriation of $174.3 million, and Cooperative Biological Research projects would receive $26.5 million, an increase over its appropriated level of $18.8 million in FY2009. Congress authorized the requested amount. At the same time, House Armed Services, in its report on the FY2010 Defense Authorization Bill (H.Rept. 111-166) called on DOD continue its efforts to strengthen the biological threat reduction programs and to pursue more interagency coordination. In addition, in recognition of the fact that biological weapons proliferation prevention has consumed a growing proportion of the CTR budget, the HASC encouraged DOD "to maintain a strong focus on ... other threat reduction challenges, including preventing the proliferation of chemical and nuclear weapons and weapons-related materials, technologies, and expertise."

For FY2011, the Obama Administration requested $209 million for Biological Threat reduction, with $184.7 million allocated to Biosafety, Biosecuirty and Threat Agent Detection and Response, and $24 million allocated to Cooperative Biological Research. Congress approved this request in the FY2011 Defense Authorization Act and the continuing resolution for FY2011 appropriations. The Obama Administration requested, and Congress approved, $259.5 million for this effort in FY2012. It has requested an additional $276.4 million in FY2013. It now refers to this project area as Cooperative Biological Engagement and, according to the budget documents, plans to use this funding to extend bio-engagement efforts and cooperative research projects outside the former Soviet states to nations in Africa.

Demilitarization Programs

Demilitarization programs included projects that encouraged Russia, Ukraine, Belarus, and Kazakhstan that were designed to convert military efforts to peaceful purposes. The International Science and Technology Center, which provides grants to Russian weapons scientists and supports cooperative research with biological weapons scientists, began with funding in this category. Funds for demilitarization also support Defense and Military contacts between officers in the United States and those in the former Soviet republics. According to DOD, these contacts between the defense establishments help "promote counter-proliferation, demilitarization, and democratic reforms."[68] This program includes representatives from Georgia, Kazakhstan, Kyrgyzstan, Moldova, Russia, Ukraine, and Uzbekistan. DOD has appropriated just over $100 million for Defense and Military contacts over the life of the CTR program; the Bush Administration requested, and Congress approved, an additional $11 million for FY2004, $8

---

[68] U.S. Department of Defense. Fiscal Year 2004/2005 Biennial Budget Estimates. Former Soviet Union Threat Reduction Appropriation. February 2003. p. 6.

million for FY2005, and $8 million for FY2006. Congress also approved the Administration's request of $8 million for FY2007. The authorizations for FY2008 and FY2009 remained the same, at $8 million. The request and authorizations have declined to $5 million in FY2010 and FY2011.

The Bush Administration added a new demilitarization program in FY2003. Through the WMD Proliferation Prevention Program, the United States has cooperated with the military establishments, internal security forces, border guards, and custom forces in Kazakhstan, Ukraine, Uzbekistan, and Azerbaijan to improve their border controls. In FY2006, Moldova joined the effort, with funding provided to begin developing its border control and monitoring systems. DOD is also helping Ukraine establish a comprehensive WMD monitoring and interdiction capability along its border with Moldova. CTR completed the radiation portal monitoring program in Uzbekistan in 2008. The program is also assisting Kazakhstan and Azerbaijan develop a comprehensive capability for WMD surveillance and interdiction along their Caspian Sea borders. These programs are intended to help these nations deter, detect, and interrupt the unauthorized movement of weapons or related materials across their borders.[69]

Congress appropriated $40 million for this program in FY2003; the Bush Administration requested $39.4 million in FY2004 but received only $29 million. It requested, and Congress authorized, an additional $40 million for FY2005 and $40.6 million in FY2006. It requested and received an additional $37.5 million for this program in FY2007. The budget request for FY2008 included $37.9 million for this program. The House approved this request, but the Senate added $14 million, for a total of $51 million. The conference committee approved nearly $48 million. It also allocated the $10 million that Congress approved for new initiatives to projects in this program area outside the former Soviet Union. For FY2009, the Bush Administration requested $50.3 million for WMD proliferation prevention programs in the former Soviet Union; Congress added $9 million, for a total of $59 million for this effort in FY2009. The Obama Administration requested, and Congress authorized, 29.1 million for this program area in FY2010. The FY2011 budget request included $26.1 million for this program area, and Congress authorized this amount in the FY2011 Defense Authorization Act. The Administration requested, and Congress approved, 28.1 million for this effort in FY2012. The Administration has requested an additional $32.4 million for this project area in FY2013.

The FY2010 budget for DOD's CTR program also includes $17 million for new CTR initiatives. Congress added $10 million to the FY2009 budget in this funding area to provide DOD with the flexibility to respond to emerging proliferation concerns in the former Soviet states and in other nations around the world. Moreover, Congress mandated that the National Academy of Sciences review the CTR problem and suggest changes that might strengthen the program.[70] DOD indicates, that, using the funds appropriated in FY2009 and FY2010, DOD expanded CTR contacts with nations outside the former Soviet Union and conducted initial biological threat reduction assessments with new countries. The Obama Administration did not request any additional funds for this program area in FY2011.

The FY2011 CTR budget added a new program area—Global Nuclear Lockdown—and requested $74.5 million for this effort. According to DOD, this funding would support efforts to secure

---

[69] Ibid., p. 10.

[70] National Academy of Sciences, *Global Security Engagement: A New Model for Cooperative Threat Reduction*, Washington, DC, April 2009.

"weapons-usable" materials in Russia and to fund "centers of excellence" outside the former Soviet Union. The budget request indicated that these centers would receive $30 million in FY2011. These centers would help DOD expand CTR support to nations outside the former Soviet Union. Congress authorized funding for this program area in the FY2011 Defense Authorization Act. However, because this program did not receive any funding in FY2010, it was not included in the funding provided through the continuing resolution. This project area was incorporated into the Global Nuclear Security project area in FY2012.

Global Nuclear Security

In the FY2012 budget request for CTR, the Obama Administration combined a number of previous program areas into a new category of Global Nuclear Security. This new area includes all the funding that had previously been allocated to nuclear weapons storage security, and some of the funding from nuclear weapons transportation security and proliferation prevention. The Administration requested $121.1 million for this program in FY2012; this compares with the FY2010 appropriation of $118.6 million and FY2011 appropriation of $164.3 million. Congress approved this amount. The Administration has requested $99.8 million for this program area in FY2013.

State Department

The State Department has played an integral role in U.S. nonproliferation and threat reduction programs since their inception. It has taken the lead in negotiating the broad agreements needed before recipient nations can receive U.S. assistance and in providing for broad policy coordination among the U.S. agencies and between the United States and recipient nations. The State Department also manages the Nonproliferation and Disarmament Fund (NDF), which it can use to help nations address problems with proliferation-prone weapons located on their territories. Congress appropriated approximately $15 million for this fund each year between 1993 and 2003. The Bush Administration requested, and Congress approved, $35 million for NDF in FY2004, $31.7 million in FY2005, and $37.5 million in FY2006. It requested $38 million in FY2007 and $30 million for FY2008, with Congress appropriating $37 million and $33.7 million for those years, respectively. The Bush Administration requested an additional $40 million for the NDF in FY2009; Congress approved this amount, and added $77 million more in the Supplemental Appropriations Acts (P.L. 111-32). The Obama Administration requested $57 million for this fund in FY2011, $30 million for FY2012, and $30 million in FY2013.

The Bush Administration indicated that it planned to use this program to expand U.S. efforts to help countries establish better accounting and control mechanisms for nuclear, chemical, and biological materials.[71] According to John Wolf, the former Assistant Secretary of State for Nonproliferation, the State Department also planed to use these funds to "focus on unanticipated opportunities to eliminate missile systems, chemical agents, and to secure orphaned radiological sources."[72] For example, funding from this program contributed to the U.S. effort to eliminate

---

[71] U.S. Senate. Committee on Foreign Relations. Testimony of John S. Wolf. Assistant Secretary of State for Nonproliferation. March 19, 2003.

[72] U.S. House. Committee on International Relations. Subcommittees on Europe and International Terrorism, Nonproliferation and Human Rights of the House Committee on International Relations Hearing on U.S. Cooperative Threat Reduction and Nonproliferation Programs. May 8, 2003.

Libya's WMD infrastructure and to help redirect weapons scientists in Libya and Iraq. Most of the funding in this program is used on projects outside the former Soviet Union.

The State Department also manages and funds the International Science and Technology Center (ISTC) in Moscow and its companion Science and Technology Center (STCU) in Kiev, Ukraine. In the FY2005 budget request, it combined these centers and the biological weapons redirect program into a new category, called Nonproliferation of WMD expertise. The State Department also manages the Export Control and Related Border Security Assistance (EXBS) Program. The following discussion provides more detail about these two program areas.[73]

Global Threat Reduction (Formerly Nonproliferation of WMD Expertise)

After the collapse of the Soviet Union in 1991, many experts feared that scientists from Russia's nuclear weapons complex might sell their knowledge to other nations seeking nuclear weapons. Many of these scientists had worked in the Soviet Union's "closed" nuclear cities, where they had enjoyed relatively high salaries and prestige, but their jobs evaporated during Russia's economic and political crises in the early 1990s. Even those scientists who retained their jobs saw their incomes decline sharply as Russia was unable to pay their salaries for months at a time.

In late 1992, the United States, Japan, the European Union, and Russia established the International Science and Technology Center (ISTC) in Moscow. Several other former Soviet states joined the center during the 1990s, and other nations, including Norway and South Korea, added their financial support. In late 1993, the United States, Canada, Sweden, and Ukraine established the Science and Technology Center in Ukraine (STCU). Several former Soviet states have also joined this center, and Japan has joined to provide financial support.

By early 2010, 39 countries were participating in the centers. According to the International Science and Technology Center in Moscow, since its inception, this facility has funded 2,702 funded proposals and awarded grants totaling $836.5 million. The funds have supported the work of more than 70,000 scientists. However, reports indicate that support for the center was waning, and funding has declined in recent years. [74] Moreover, the future of the center is uncertain because, in August 2010, Russia's President Medvedev announced that Russia was withdrawing from participation in the center. This may not affect the center's ability to grant funds to Russian scientists, but it could alter the operations of the programs.

The centers fund scientists who have worked on nuclear, chemical, and biological weapons, but they have, historically, focused on nuclear scientists, with many projects going to those who work at institutes in the closed nuclear cities. The State Department estimates that about half of the participants are senior scientists, which means the programs may have reached a significant portion of the estimated 30,000 to 70,000 senior scientists and engineers in the Soviet nuclear complex. However, most of these scientists spend fewer than 50 days per year on projects funded by the science centers. In the remainder of the time, most continue to work at their primary jobs.

---

[73] For a more details see *Controlling Nuclear Warheads and Materials: A Report Card and Action Plan*, by Matthew Bunn et al. Project on Managing the Atom. March 2003.

[74] "Budget Cuts Threaten Support Program for Former Soviet Weapons Experts," *Global Security Newswire*, June 19, 2009.

In addition, some of the grants go to research institutes in Russia, rather than directly to scientists, and some of these funds may be used for administrative or management purposes. Nevertheless, the income earned from even short-term research projects may undermine incentives these individuals might otherwise encounter to sell their knowledge to potential proliferant nations.

The Science Centers also sponsor a Partners Program, through which private industry, universities, and other government agencies can provide funding for and establish contacts with former Soviet scientists. The program started small, with about 30 partners and $5 million in projects in 1997; it had grown to 166 partners supporting over 100 projects worth $31 million in 2002. This represented one quarter of the grant funding provided by the science centers in 2002.[75] In FY2009, the Partner Program had grown to include more than 430 partners, and it provided $9.5 million to support 34 projects.

Between 1994 and 2009, the ISTC in Moscow had received more than $803 million in funding from its participating nations, with the United States providing about $220 million of this total. The United States has also provides support through the ISTC to the Biological Weapons Redirection Program.[76] This program provides research grants to Russian biotechnology institutes to redirect scientists to commercial, agricultural, and public health projects. The State Department collaborates with several other U.S. agencies in this program.[77] In recent years, it has begun to shift grant funding away from Russia's nuclear scientists to biological and chemical weapons scientists, thus re-naming the program the Bio-Chem Redirection program, and to scientists from other former Soviet states. Further, it expects this decline in funding to force the ISTC to focus more on "graduating scientists" from U.S. assistance to projects with more commercial viability.[78] The State Department operates a third program within this category, known as the Bio Industry Initiative (BII). This initiative, which began in 2002, seeks to help Russia reconfigure its large-scale former BW-related facilities so that they can perform peaceful research issues such as infectious diseases. The Global Threat Reduction program has also expanded beyond the borders of the former Soviet Union, with programs designed to engage scientists in Iraq and Libya.

For FY2004, the Bush Administration requested $59 million for the science centers and BW redirection programs, and received about 50.2 million. It did not identify the precise funding for either of the two. In its FY2005 budget, it requested $50.5 million, with about $30.5 million going to the science centers, $17 million going to the Bio-Chem Redirect program, and $3 million going to the BII.[79] Congress approved the Bush Administration's budget request for this program area in FY2006, appropriating $52.6 million. However, a declining proportion of the budget is likely to be spent on programs in the former Soviet Union, as this program is expanding to help redirect scientists in Libya and Iraq.

The Bush Administration requested 22.7 million for the Science Centers in its FY2007 budget. It also requested $17 million for the Bio-Chem Redirect program and $13 million for the Bio-Industry Initiative. This total of $52.7 million will be spent primarily in the former Soviet states. The Administration has requested $2.5 million for the scientist redirection program in Iraq and $1

---

[75] Ibid.

[76] Ibid.

[77] For more details, see CRS Report RL31368, *Preventing Proliferation of Biological Weapons: U.S. Assistance to the Former Soviet States*, by Michelle Stem Cook and Amy F. Woolf.

[78] U.S. Department of State. FY2004 Congressional Budget Justification for Foreign Operations. p. 370.

[79] U.S. Department of State. FY2006 Congressional Budget Justification for Foreign Operations. p. 135.

million for the program in Libya.[80] It requested a total of $53.5 million for these two program areas in FY2008 and $64 million in FY2009. The Obama Administration requested approximately $68 million for these programs in FY2010. The FY2011 and FY2012 budgets each included $69 million for the Global Threat Reduction Program. The Administration has requested $64 million for FY2013.

Analysts have raised numerous questions about the science center programs. One of the first critiques came from the General Accounting Office, in a study published in 1995. GAO found that some scientists who received grants from the ISTC "may also continue to be employed by institutes engaged in weapons work."[81] GAO interpreted this finding to mean that the centers had not succeeded in redirecting weapons scientists to peaceful endeavors. Other critics of the CTR program claimed that GAO's findings indicated that, by supporting Russian weapons scientists, U.S. funds were supporting Russian weapons programs. The State Department disputed both of these conclusions, noting that the grants from the ISTC were intended to supplement, not replace, the scientists' income from work in other institutes. And, in the years since this report, the State Department has enhanced its auditing procedures to ensure that ISTC grants support the assigned projects and do not support work on Russian weapons.

Analysts have also noted that the ISTC and STCU do not have enough money to support full pay for a significant number of scientists. Consequently, some have questioned whether the centers achieve their objective of keeping these scientists away from nations or groups seeking weapons of mass destruction. Others, however, note that, even if the financial support is less than complete, the cooperation with Russian institutes, and the promise of a fairly steady stream of funding, helps build relationships and draw these institutes into the "western orbit."[82] To address this problem, some have suggested that, instead of providing short-term grants, the centers should focus on projects that will lead to the long-term redirection of scientists out of weapons work. The State Department seems to agree with this approach, with its growing reliance on the Partners Program and its acknowledged need to transition Russia's nuclear scientists to more commercially viable projects.

Export Control and Related Border Security Assistance

Many view the potential for smuggling or illegal exports of materials and technology from the former Soviet Union as a key proliferation concern. The collapse of political control along the Soviet borders, along with incentives created by the weakness in the economies of the newly independent states, contributes to this growing concern. The State Department's Export Control and Related Border Security Assistance (EXBS) program helps the former Soviet states and other nations improve their ability to interdict nuclear smuggling and stop the illicit trafficking of all materials for weapons of mass destruction, along with dual use goods and technologies. The

---

[80] U.S. Department of State. U.S. Department of State. FY2005 Congressional Budget Justification for Foreign Operations. pp. 135, 140-144.

[81] U.S. General Accounting Office. *Weapons of Mass Destruction, Reducing the Threat From the Former Soviet Union: An Update.* GAO/NSIAD-95-165, June 1995. Washington, DC. p. 27.

[82] *Controlling Nuclear Warheads and Materials: A Report Card and Action Plan*, by Matthew Bunn et al. Project on Managing the Atom. March 2003.

EXBS program currently has projects underway in more than 30 nations and is expanding its reach around the globe.[83]

When designing a nation-specific plan for border control assistance, the United States seeks to address four key areas. First, if needed, it helps the recipient nation establish the legal and regulatory basis for effective export controls. It then helps the nation develop appropriate export licensing procedures and practices. Third, the United States helps the recipient establish and enhance effective enforcement capabilities. When needed, it provides the recipient with detection and interdiction equipment and training. Finally, the United States helps establish procedures that promote effective interaction between government and industry so that business entities in the recipient nation will abide by the laws and regulations of the new export control regime.

The State Department also provides support to border control efforts in DOD's CTR program and the DOE's nonproliferation program. It seeks to coordinate these and other U.S. efforts to identify and stop the smuggling of nuclear, chemical, and biological weapons or materials. Analysts inside and outside the government have questioned, however, whether the coordination has been effective. Consequently, the National Security Council is leading an effort to develop a government-wide strategic plan for interdiction assistance, which includes but is not limited to export assistance, that might help stop the smuggling of weapons of mass destruction.

Between FY1998 and FY2002, the State Department allocated $146 million to the EXBS program for nations in and around the former Soviet Union. Approximately $100 million of this amount was allocated to Georgia for its border security program. Funding for border security in the rest of the former Soviet states was around $5-$7 million per year, until the State Department added $24.7 million from the FY2002 supplemental appropriations. In FY2003, the State Department requested around $17 million for the EXBS program, with an additional $15 million allocated to the Georgia Border Security Program. Funding declined in FY2004; the Bush Administration requested $13.9 million for EXBS and an additional $15 million for the Georgia Border Security program. In FY2005, the Bush Administration requested a total of $38 million for EXBS, although only around $19 million was allocated to projects in nations in and around the former Soviet Union. An additional $11.5 million was allocated to "global" efforts, with the remaining $7 million allocated to projects in other nations around the world. This trend continued in FY2006 and FY2007. The budget request for the EXBS program equals $44.4 million. Congress approved $43.4 million. However, only around $8.5 million of this amount will go to projects in nations around the former Soviet Union. A far greater amount, around $19 million, is allocated to nations in other regions such as South Asia and the Near East. The remainder is allocated to global programs, such as the provision of advisors and equipment and the development of global regional export controls. For FY2007, the Bush Administration requested $45.050 million for the EXBS program; less than $6 million would go to states that were once a part of the Soviet Union. For FY2008, the total request was $41.3 million, but only around 4.5 million was allocated to states of the former Soviet Union. For FY2009, the request was for $42.1 million, with less than $4 million going to states of the former Soviet Union. The Obama Administration requested $55 million for EXBS in FY2010, but, again, less than $4 million of that funding will go to nations in the former Soviet Union. The State Department requested $61 million for this program in FY2011 and FY2012, but, again, only a fraction is allocated to nations

---

[83] U.S. Senate. Committee on Foreign Relations. Testimony of John S. Wolf. Assistant Secretary of State for Nonproliferation. March 19, 2003.

that were a part of the former Soviet Union. The FY2013 budget request includes $55 million for EXBS.

Department of Energy

The Department of Energy has contributed to U.S. threat reduction and nonproliferation assistance to the former Soviet states from the start, when CTR included a small amount of funding for materials control and protection. Officials from DOE participated, along with their counterparts at DOD, in early efforts to outline projects and reach agreement with Russian officials on assistance to secure nuclear materials. But these government-to-government negotiations proceeded slowly, in part because Russia's nuclear energy ministry—known as Minatom at the time—was less open to cooperation than the Ministry of Defense. Consequently, projects at facilities that housed nuclear materials did not begin until 1994. In a parallel effort that sought to reduce these delays, experts from the U.S. nuclear laboratories, which are a part of DOE, also began less formal contacts with their counterparts in Russia to identify and solve safety and security problems at Russian facilities. Together, these government-to-government and lab-to-lab projects evolved into an effort to apply Material Protection, Control and Accounting (MPC&A) techniques to Russian facilities.

The MPC&A program began with less than $3 million in FY1993. This amount grew to $73 million in FY1995. In FY1996, DOE assumed budgetary and management responsibility for the program. DOE also initiated a second program, the Initiatives for Proliferation Prevention, which sought to provide employment opportunities for scientists and engineers from Russia's nuclear weapons complex. In the latter half of the 1990s, DOE expanded these efforts and added several other programs to its nonproliferation assistance. These programs are now managed by DOE's National Nuclear Security Administration (NNSA). The discussion below summarizes the objectives and achievements of many of these efforts.[84]

International Nuclear Materials Protection and Cooperation

The International Nuclear Materials Protection and Cooperation program seeks to "secure nuclear weapons and weapons-usable nuclear materials by upgrading security at nuclear sites, by consolidating these materials to sites where installation of enhanced security systems have already been completed, and by improving nuclear smuggling detection capabilities at international borders."[85] The MPC&A program[86] addresses the first of these objectives. The Materials Consolidation and Conversion Program addresses the second, and the Second Line of Defense (SLD) and Megaports programs address the third. Each of these is discussed below.

---

[84] As was the case with the summaries of DOD and State Department programs, these descriptions do not cover all DOE programs. A complete description of the programs funded under DOE's Defense Nuclear Nonproliferation Budget can be found in DOE's budget documents. See U.S. Department of Energy. FY2006 Congressional Budget Request. Detailed Budget Justifications. February 2005. pp. 481-497.

[85] U.S. Department of Energy. FY2004 Congressional Budget Request. Detailed Budget Justifications. February 2003. p. 623.

[86] This program area included, for a short time, an effort to identify and secure radiological sources that could be used to make radiological dispersion devices. In the FY2005 budget request, this initiative is combined with two others in a single initiative known as "International Nuclear and Radiological Cleanout." See 2005 DOE Budget Rollout. Remarks by Secretary of Energy Spencer Abraham. February 2, 2004, Washington, DC.

MPC&A Funding

The budget for MPC&A grew rapidly during the 1990s, reaching $169 million in FY2001, the last year of the Clinton Administration. The Bush Administration, in its budget request for FY2002, reduced funding for the MPC&A program to $138.8 million, in part because it believed that the program had enough unexpended funds from prior years to carry on with less funding. Its first budget also shifted money from Defense Nuclear Nonproliferation Programs to U.S. nuclear weapons programs. Congress objected to this reduction, and both the Senate and House Appropriations Committees, in the Energy and Water Appropriations bills for FY2002, restored funding to the FY2001 level. Furthermore, Congress added $150 million in a supplemental appropriations bill passed at the end of 2001, after the September 11 attacks had raised new concerns about the potential threat that terrorists might seek to acquire nuclear materials from insecure facilities in Russia. The Bush Administration allocated much of this new funding to the Second Line of Defense and Radiological Dispersion Devices. But the Bush Administration did increase its budget request for MPC&A in FY2003, to $223 million, so that it could accelerate the installation of comprehensive upgrades and material consolidation and conversion efforts.[87] The Bush Administration requested $227 million for these efforts for FY2004; Congress approved $260 million, adding $5 million for "high priority" activities and $28 million for an initiative under the Second Line of Defense Program (described below).

The Bush Administration requested $238 million for MPC&A in FY2005. The reduction from FY2004 to FY2005 reflected, in part, the completion of physical security upgrades at Russian Navy warhead storage sites.[88] In the conference report on the FY2005 Defense Authorization Bill (H.Rept. 108-767; P.L. 108-375), Congress authorized the full amount requested by the President. The House had reduced that amount by around $10 million, citing delays in the program caused by Russia's refusal to allow the United States access to some facilities, but the Senate prevailed in conference. The Appropriations Committee added $84 million to the MPC&A program, for a total of $322 million. The conference report accompanying the Consolidated Appropriations Act, 2005 (H.Rept. 108-792; P.L. 108-447), notes that this added funding should be used to accelerate efforts to secure nuclear weapons sites and nuclear materials production sites in Russia.[89]

The Bush Administration requested $343.4 million for these programs in FY2006. Nearly $100 million of this total was allocated to the Second Line of Defense and Megaports Initiative, leaving approximately $245 million to secure nuclear materials in Russia. In the FY2006 Defense Authorization Act (P.L. 109-163, H.Rept. 109-360), Congress added approximately $20 million to this total, in part to accelerate warhead security work at the Strategic Rocket Force facilities. The Energy and Water Appropriations Committee added $83.6 million to this portion of the DOE budget, so that DOE could pursue "new opportunities in warhead security work with Russia.

In the FY2007 budget, the Bush Administration requested $413.2 million for MPC&A. Although this exceeds the Administration's request for FY2006, it falls below the appropriated amount of $422.7 million. In addition, it includes $124 million for Second Line of Defense and Megaports, leaving $298.7 million to secure nuclear materials in Russia. Within this total, as is noted below, the Administration shifted money among the different project areas, as some ongoing projects

---

[87] U.S. House. Committee on Appropriations. Statement of Spencer Abraham, Secretary of Energy. March 6, 2002.

[88] Hoehn, William. *Preliminary Analysis of U.S. Department of Energy's Fiscal Year 2005 Nonproliferation Budget Request.* RANSAC. February 4. 2004.

[89] Congressional Record. November 19, 2004. H10558.

---

accelerate and others move toward their conclusion. Specifically, the budget indicated that work at the Rosatom complex, which houses most of Russia's nuclear weapons materials, would be reduced, while sustainment activities would increase. Congress did not accept some of these changes, appropriating a total of $472.7 million for this program area and shifting money among the budget areas, as is noted in more detail below.

The FY2008 budget request sought a total of $371.7 million for the MPC&A program areas, with $119.3 million going to the Second Line of Defense and Megaports initiatives. This leaves $251.8 million for the efforts to secure nuclear warheads and materials in Russia. The DOE budget request also reflects continuing declines in the MPC&A budget in the outyears, as many of the MPC&A upgrades to storage facilities are completed and the program switches to sustainment activities. DOE also noted that Russia has added some Rosatom sites to its list of sites in need of upgrades; if these are approved, they would also be added to budget and work effort after FY2008.

Congress increased, in some cases significantly, funding for the MPC&A programs in the FY2008 Defense Authorization Act (H.Rept. 110-477) and the FY2008 Omnibus Appropriations Bill (H.R. 2764). For example, the House version of the FY2008 Defense Authorization Bill (H.R. 1585) included $401 million for MPC&A, which essentially incorporates $30 million from the FY2008 Supplemental request into the Authorization Bill. The Senate, for its part, added only $10 million, authorizing $381.8 million. The conference committee added $30 million, with most of this going to the Second Line of Defense program. On the other hand, the House Energy and Water Development Subcommittee of the House Appropriations Committee more than doubled the request for funding for MPC&A, providing $831.8 million (H.Rept. 110-185). The committee noted that this program is on the "front line" in the global war on terror because it seeks to protect the United States against a terrorist using a nuclear device on U.S. soil. As is noted below, the committee added funding in several areas to accelerate work at Russia's nuclear materials facilities and warhead storage facilities, and to expand the Second Line of Defense and Megaports programs. The Senate Energy and Water Appropriations Bill, in contrast, added only $20 million to this program area (S.Rept. 110-127). The Omnibus Appropriations Bill for FY2008 includes $624 million MPC&A, with $136 million going to Second Line of Defense and $130.8 million for Megaports (these are described in more detail below).

The President's budget for FY2009 requested $429 million for MPC&A programs; Congress added $22 million to this project area. As discussed in more detail below, the budget request for most of the project areas fell sharply below the amount appropriated in FY2008. These declines, in most cases, reflected the fact that, with the added funding appropriated in FY2008, many of the ongoing projects are nearing completion. The Obama Administration requested $552.3 million for this project area in FY2010, a significant increase over the amount appropriated in FY2009. The request included a significant increase of $92 million, for a total of $194 million, for the Megaports program, but also allocated added funding to several of the efforts to secure nuclear warheads and materials in Russia. Congress authorized $592 million for these programs in FY2010, but appropriated only $572 million. President Obama requested $590 million for these programs in FY2011, with $265 million going to the Second Line of Defense and Megaports. Congress approved this request in the FY2011 Defense Authorization Act, but, with funding held to FY2010 levels in the continuing resolution, these programs have received 572.1 million in appropriations for FY2011.

The Obama Administration requested $571.6 million for this program area in FY2012; Congress appropriated $569.9 million. Within this total, $132.7 million was allocated to the Megaports initiative, leaving $437.2 million to secure warheads and materials in Russia. The Obama Administration has requested $311 million for this program area in FY2013. As is discussed below, most of the reductions reflect completion of materials protection projects. There are also significant reductions in Second Line of Defense and Megaports, as projects in these areas near completion.

Between FY1993 and FY2012, Congress appropriated nearly $5 billion for the MPC&A program. With the exception of approximately $1 billion for the Second Line of Defense and Megaports programs, these funds were allocated to efforts to improve security at nuclear warhead and nuclear material storage facilities in Russia. NNSA has identified 105 nuclear sites, with 243 buildings, that may need assistance in improving their security systems. According to NNSA, these sites contain approximately 600 metric tons of nuclear materials, enough for around 41,000 nuclear warheads. Within this total, 63 sites belong to the Ministry of Defense, (52 warhead storage site and 11 Navy fuel storage sites), 11 are a part of the Minatom (now known as Rosatom)[90] weapons complex, and 31 are civilian sites. More than 80% of these materials are located at the Rosatom/Minatom sites.[91]

MPC&A Projects

DOE provides MPC&A assistance at Russian facilities in two phases. First, it installs rapid upgrades that are designed to delay unauthorized access to the storage facilities. These may include the installation of hardened doors and windows, locks and keys to control access, perimeter fences, and moveable barriers at entry points. The second phase provides comprehensive upgrades that are tailored to meet the security needs at each individual facility. These may include monitoring and detection systems, the relocation of guard forces, the consolidation of materials, central alarm systems, and electronic access control systems. DOE has helped improve security at sites that house considerably more than half of the former Soviet Union's 600 metric tons of weapons-usable nuclear materials.[92] In 2006, DOE altered the way in which it measures progress in these programs, focusing on the percentage of facilities that had received upgrades, rather than the percentage of materials that were captured by the upgrades. By the end of 2006, DOE had completed rapid upgrades at about 81% of the 215 facilities housing this material and comprehensive upgrades at about 63% of these facilities.[93] DOE reported that, by September of 2007, it had completed upgrades at nearly 90%, or 193, of the buildings. Moreover, in recent years, some of the funding in this program area has gone to support security upgrades at nuclear facilities outside the former Soviet Union.

---

[90] Russia reorganized its government entities, beginning in March 2004. MINATOM, the Ministry of Atomic Energy, was redesignated as the Federal Agency for Atomic Energy, or Rosatom. Rosatom is still the primary agency responsible for nuclear weapons. See Matthew Bouldin. Updated Analysis. Russian Government Restructuring and the Future of WMD Threat Reduction Cooperation. RANSAC. May 2004.

[91] U.S. Department of Energy. FY2004 Congressional Budget Request. Detailed Budget Justifications. February 2003. p. 625.

[92] U.S. Senate. Committee on Foreign Relations. Statement of Ambassador Linton Brooks. Administrator, NNSA. June 15, 2004. See also, U.S. General Accounting Office. Weapons of Mass Destruction. Additional Russian Cooperation Needed to Facilitate U.S. Efforts to Improve Security at Russian Sites. GA)-03-482. Washington, March 2003. p. 4. See also, U.S. Senate, Committee on Armed Services. Statement of Paul M. Longsworth. Deputy Administrator for Defense Nuclear Nonproliferation. March 10, 2004. (Herein after referred to as Longsworth Testimony.)

[93] Bunn, Matthew. Securing the Bomb2007. Project on Managing the Atom. Commissioned by the Nuclear Threat Initiative. September 2007. p. 65.

When the upgrades are complete, DOE plans to continue "sustainability efforts" to ensure that the upgrades remain effective in the long term. This program, titled National Programs and Sustainability, seeks to create regulations, reporting requirements, training and maintenance facilities, and other infrastructure components to ensure that Russia can continue to operate its new security systems.[94]

Navy Complex

DOE has provided assistance to Russia's navy by improving security at 39 naval nuclear warhead storage sites and 11 nuclear fuel storage sites. These sites house approximately 60 metric tons of weapons-useable nuclear materials and 4,000 nuclear warheads. According to DOE, it had completed rapid and comprehensive upgrades at all naval nuclear fuel storage sites by the end of 2004, and had completed the comprehensive upgrades at the last two warhead sites in FY2006. The FY2006 budget request included $6.5 million for this program area, a reduction that reflected the completion of much of the work. However, in response to the U.S. and Russian commitment at the Bratislava summit to accelerate work on warhead storage security, Congress approved $16 million for the navy complex sites in FY2006. The Bush Administration requested an additional $17.3 million in FY2007; the House and Senate Armed Services Committees approved this request. The FY2008 budget requested, and Congress appropriated, $13.4 million for this project area. The FY2009 budget request included $16.4 million. These funds, and the funds appropriated in FY2007 and FY2008, will be used to provide "sustainability support" at the sites, which includes training and site level maintenance on the equipment at the sites, as the upgrades were completed at by the end of 2008. The FY2010 budget request for this program area included $33.9 million, with the focus on additional support for training and sustainability. Congress appropriated 33.8 million for FY2010.

NNSA requested, and Congress appropriated, $34.3 million for the Navy Complex programs in FY2011. The Administration requested, and Congress approved, an additional $33.7 million for these programs in FY2012. It has also requested $39.9 million in FY2013. These funds will support sustainability and training programs at the sites and will provide for the replacement of outdated security equipment at eight sites.

Strategic Rocket Forces

DOE has completed security upgrades at warhead storage sites for Russia's strategic rocket forces. The United States approved upgrades at 25 sites on 11 SRF bases; work on these sites was completed in late October 2007, nearly two years ahead of schedule.[95] It is upgraded security at nine sites under the command of the 12th Main Directorate, the branch of Russia's Ministry of Defense responsible for warhead security and maintenance. It completed the work on upgrades at these sites in FY2009. DOE requested $47.5 million to continue these activities in FY2006. The Defense Authorization Bill (P.L. 109-163) increased this total by $10 million, and the Energy and Water Appropriations Bill increased it by $86 million. Consequently, the FY2006 appropriation for this project area was $120.2 million. The Bush Administration requested, and Congress approved, $129.3 million for this project area in FY2007. The FY2008 budget request included

---

[94] For more details see U.S. Department of Energy. FY2004 Congressional Budget Request. Detailed Budget Justifications. February 2003. p. 655.

[95] Chivers, C.J. Securing Russian Nuclear Missiles? U.S. Is Set to Say "Done." *New York Times*, October 31, 2007.

$91.5 million for this project area. The decline in the request reflected the fact that the accelerated pace of the last few years had brought some of the sites close to completion. Congress, however, appropriated $121.9 million for this project area. The FY2009 budget requested only $53.6 million, but Congress appropriated only $34.4 million. The decline again reflects the completion of most of the work on upgrades and a shift to sustainment activities at all these sites. The FY2010 budget, however, requested, and Congress appropriated, $48.6 million for this program area, with a planned expansion of the sustainment activities. The FY2011 budget request increased this amount to $51.4 million. Congress authorized this request, but the appropriation, funded through the continuing resolution, equals the FY2010 level of $48.6 million. The Administration again increased its request in FY2012, and Congress approved, $59.1 million for this program. These funds supported sustainability and training programs at 23 SRF sites and 3 sites of the 12th Main Directorate.

The Administration has requested $8.3 million for these projects in FY2013. According to the Administration, the decrease from FY2012 reflects the completion of the sustainability support efforts in FY2012. The remaining funding will support for 3 training and maintenance centers and will allow for the replacement of outdated security equipment at up to 11 sites.

Weapons Material Protection (Formerly Rosatom Weapons Complex)

Work at Russia's nuclear weapons complex, managed by Rosatom, consists of seven sites and four "Enterprises of the Nuclear Weapons Complex" in Russia's nine closed nuclear cities. The buildings in this complex house around 500 metric tons of "highly attractive" weapons-useable materials.[96] DOE has completed rapid upgrades on buildings that house about 60% of these materials and comprehensive upgrades on buildings that house another 25% of these materials. By the end of 2006, DOE had completed work on 92 buildings in the Rosatom complex. The pace of work at these facilities has accelerated, with increased funding and increased cooperation from Russia, during the past few years. DOE hopes to install security upgrades at all these facilities by 2008. DOE has stated that an access agreement signed in 2001 has "allowed significant access and acceleration of physical protection systems ... at these large facilities."[97] In addition, Secretary of Energy Spencer Abraham reported that, in numerous meetings with Russia's Minister of Atomic Energy, Alexander Rumyantsev, he worked "to accelerate and expand our programs" and to "clear away the bureaucratic obstacles."[98]

The FY2006 budget requested $86 million for this program area, a steep increase from the $18.7 million appropriated in FY2004 and a slight reduction from the $88 million appropriated in FY2005. Congress approved this request. The FY2007 budget requested only $56.5 million for this program area. DOE noted that the reduction reflected the completion of many of the projects that were accelerated over the past few years. The House and Senate Armed Services Committees both approved this request. The House Energy and Water Development Appropriations Committee, however, increased this request by $65 million, for a total of $121.5 million for FY2007; the final appropriation was $85 million. The FY2008 budget requested $60.1 million for

---

[96] Ibid. p. 639.

[97] U.S. Department of Energy. FY2004 Congressional Budget Request. Detailed Budget Justifications. February 2003. p. 639.

[98] "The FY2004 Nonproliferation Budget: Supporting the Ten Principles for Nuclear and Radiological Materials Security." Remarks by Energy Secretary Spencer Abraham. Center for Strategic and International Studies. Washington, DC. February 10, 2003.

this project area. Congress again increased the funding, appropriating $79.1 million. The FY2009 budget request showed a steep decline, with the Bush Administration requesting only $32.3 million. This reduction, again, reflects the completion of many projects that were accelerated over the last few years. Congress, however, appropriated $56.1 million, and, in FY2010, the Obama Administration requested $71.5 million. Congress appropriated this amount. DOE indicated that, in FY2009, the majority of the continuing work would occur at the sites at Mayak, Arzamas-16, and Chelyabinsk-70. The added funding in FY2010 would go to fund upgrades at facilities that had recently been added to the program and to replace and retrofit equipment that had reached the end of its service life at facilities that have already received upgrades.

The NNSA budget request for FY2011 included $105.3 million for the Rosatom complex. This request would fund upgrades at sites that were added to the program after the Bratislava agreement in 2004. The budget documents indicate that DOE planned to make significant efforts, in FY2011, toward "implementing a comprehensive MPC&A sustainability effort at these sites. This funding would also support projects outside Russia, in other former Soviet states. Congress authorized this request in the FY2011 Defense Authorization Act. The Obama Administration requested, and Congress approved, $80.7 million for the Rosatom complex in FY2012. This funding will support, among other projects, the start of comprehensive MPC&A upgrades at 10 new buildings that store and process weapons-usable nuclear materials.

The Obama Administration has requested $47 million for this project area in FY2013. The reduction from FY2012 reflects the fact that many of the ongoing projects that provide security upgrades will be completed during the year.

Civilian Nuclear Sites

DOE has assisted with the installation of security upgrades at 31 civilian nuclear sites throughout the former Soviet Union. These are mainly research facilities that operate nuclear reactors. According to DOE, these sites contain around 40 metric tons of weapons-useable materials. DOE has already completed rapid and comprehensive upgrades at most of these facilities; it had planned to complete the comprehensive upgrades at facilities housing the final 5% of nuclear materials during FY2006, but this schedule slipped, and they are now due to be completed in FY2008. It also plans to expand its efforts to secure weapons-useable nuclear materials at civilian facilities outside the former Soviet Union. DOE has requested, and Congress approved, $47 million for this effort in FY2006, a substantial increase over the $14.6 million appropriated in FY2005. The Bush Administration requested only $21.2 million for this program area in FY2007. DOE noted that the decrease reflects the completion of initial upgrades at a facility outside the former Soviet Union. Congress, however, appropriated $52.7 million for this program area. The Bush Administration has requested $22.2 million for this effort in FY2008, but Congress again increased the funding, appropriating $54.2 million. The Bush Administration requested $34.5 million for FY2009, and Congress approved this request. DOE indicated that this funding would help foster "site capabilities" to operate and maintain the equipment and will provide sustainability support at the 19 sites with completed upgrades.

The Obama Administration requested $43.5 million for this program area in FY2010; Congress increased this amount to $63.5 million. The Administration requested, and Congress approved, $59 million for this effort in FY2011 and $59.1 million in FY2012. The Administration has requested an additional $60.1 million in FY2013. As with the other projects in this program area, much of the funding will go to sustainability efforts. Congress authorized the Administration's request.

Material Consolidation and Conversion

In addition to securing sites that house nuclear materials, the MPC&A program is providing Russia and the other former Soviet states with assistance in consolidating these materials in fewer facilities and converting them to forms that might be less attractive to nations seeking materials for nuclear weapons. By the end of FY2003, DOE had planned to remove nuclear materials from about 40% of the 55 buildings that will eventually be cleared of this material. It also plans to convert about 17 metric tons of highly enriched uranium and low enriched uranium by 2012. DOE requested $28 million for this effort in its budget for FY2006. Congress added $10 million to this request in the FY2006 Defense Authorization Act (P.L. 109-163). The Administration requested an additional $16.8 million for this program area in FY2007. DOE reports that the decrease is due to a slow-down in the availability of highly enriched uranium, which is blended down to low enriched uranium with funds in this area. The Senate Armed Services Committee approved this request, but the House increased it to $21.8 million. The final amount approved for FY2007 was $27.7 million, reflecting increases in the appropriations process. The FY2008 budget request included $19.7 million for this project area; Congress appropriated this amount. The budget request for FY2009 included $20.9 million for this program area. For FY2010, the Obama Administration reduced the request to $13.6 million. Congress approved this request. In FY2011, DOE sought, and Congress authorized, $13.9 million for this effort. Congress also approved the Administration's request of 14.3 million for FY2012. The Administration has requested an additional $17 million for FY2013. It plans to continue to use this funding to continue converting special nuclear materials a form that is less attractive for proliferation to nations or groups seeking nuclear weapons.

National Programs and Sustainability

The MPC&A budget also supports an effort to build an infrastructure within Russia that can operate effectively and be sustained in the recipient nations after the initial and comprehensive upgrades are complete. These efforts include developing regulations, inspection capabilities, site safeguards, security programs, and other accounting capabilities. The program will operate regional technical support facilities that can repair and maintain equipment and develop training programs for participants. In the FY2005 budget request, DOE reduced funding for this initiative from $41 million appropriated in FY2005 to $30 million, continuing a trend of preceding years. DOE noted in 2004 that funding in this area had declined because DOE altered it priorities to support increased funding for MPC&A activities in countries outside the former Soviet Union.[99] The Bush Administration sought to reverse this decline in FY2007, with a request of $48.1 million, but Congress appropriated only $29.7 million. The Administration requested $45.6 million in FY2008, and Congress appropriated nearly $70 million. The Bush Administration requested $59.3 million for FY2009, and Congress appropriated $54.9 million. The Obama Administration has requested $68.5 million for sustainability programs in FY2010, and Congress approved this amount. The Obama Administration requested, and Congress authorized, $61 million for this effort in FY2011. The Administration requested, and Congress approved, $60.9 million for FY2012. The Administration has requested an additional $46.2 million for FY2013.

---

[99] Hoehn, William. *Preliminary Analysis of U.S. Department of Energy's Fiscal Year 2005 Nonproliferation Budget Request*. RANSAC. February 4. 2004

Radiological Dispersion Devices

In the wake of the September 11 attacks, many analysts have expressed growing concerns about the possibility that terrorists might acquire nuclear materials that could be used in a "dirty bomb." Although such a device would not explode with a nuclear yield, it could, nonetheless, spread radiological debris across a wide area. Many nations around the world have nuclear materials at research facilities, hospitals, or power plants that could be used in a dirty bomb. But most analysts agree that the states of the former Soviet Union pose a greater threat in this regard, particularly since the Soviet Union left devices with radioactive materials scattered across its territory. According to Spencer Abraham, the Secretary of Energy, "more attention is being paid to the risks associated with the misuse of radiological materials" because they are much "more abundant and much less secure" than weapons-grade materials.[100] Consequently, DOE developed a program to identify these sites, set priorities, and begin security upgrades. This program received its initial funding in FY2002, with $20 million allocated from the $150 million Congress added to the MPC&A program in the Supplemental Appropriations (P.L. 107-206) passed after the September 11 attacks.

DOE identified 35 nuclear waste sites in Russia and the other former Soviet states that posed a threat for the theft or sale of nuclear materials. These states also have radiological sources at agricultural research institutes, research reactors, medical facilities, intelligence sites, and defense facilities.[101] DOE is also working with the International Atomic Energy Agency (IAEA) to identify and secure facilities that may house these materials in other nations. In FY2005, DOE received around $24.8 million for this effort. In the FY2006 budget, DOE moved this program to the Global Threat Reduction Initiative portion of its program and requested an additional $24 million. It requested $18.3 million for International radiological threat reduction in FY2007 and $6 million in FY2008; this program no longer focuses exclusively on sites in the former Soviet Union.

Second Line of Defense

Through its Second Line of Defense Program, DOE contributes to U.S. efforts to help the former Soviet states detect and intercept attempts to smuggle nuclear materials out of the country. DOE has begun to install radiation detection equipment systems at strategic "transit and border sites." By the end of FY2006, the program had installed equipment at more than 150 sites and planned to add 51 more sites in FY2007. According to DOE, the core program has equipped 161 sites in Russia with radiation detection equipment and hopes to equip a total of 370 sites in Russia with this equipment by 2011. DOE also plans to provide training and communications equipment to border control agents to help them implement the plan. The core program has also provided equipment to 69 sites outside of Russia. This program began in FY1998 and received less than $3 million per year for several years. However, the budget increased to $46 million, and the effort expanded significantly with funding provided under the FY2002 supplemental appropriations (P.L. 107-206). DOE requested, and Congress approved, $24 million for the core program of Second Line of Defense in FY2006.

---

[100] Remarks by Spencer Abraham, Secretary of Energy. Carnegie Endowment for International Peace. International Nonproliferation Conference. November 14 , 2002

[101] U.S. Department of Energy. FY2004 Congressional Budget Request. Detailed Budget Justifications. February 2003. p. 649.

Congress also added $28 million in FY2004 for a project known as the Megaports initiative. This project is developing and deploying radiation detectors for use at the largest foreign seaports that handle about 70% of the container traffic headed for the United States.[102] Megaports is designed "to detect the trafficking of nuclear or radioactive materials in the world's busiest seaports." According to former Secretary of Energy Abraham, DOE hopes to install detection equipment at seaports around the globe. At the end of 2008, according to DOE, the Megaports program had completed work at 23 ports and planned to complete work at 5 more ports in 2009. The Administration requested $15 million for this program in FY2005 and $73.9 million for this program in FY2006. This funding is included in International Nuclear Materials and Protection portion of the budget, even though it is not intended for use in the former Soviet Union. As a result, it is not included in this report's DOE totals for nonproliferation projects in the former Soviet Union. It is worth noting, however, that the increase in Megaports for FY2006 exceeded the increase in the entire International Nuclear Materials and Protection portion of the budget, signaling a shift in funding out of the former Soviet Union and into projects in other nations.

The Bush Administration requested a total of $124 million for Second Line of Defense and Megaports in FY2007. This was an increase of $27 million over the combined budget for the two programs in FY2006. But it also contained a significant shift, with $84 million allocated to Second Line of Defense and only $40 million allocated to Megaports. The increase in SLD reflects the acceleration of efforts to install radiation detection equipment at sites in the Caucuses region, while the decrease in Megaports is attributed to the completion of the installation of radiation detection equipment at five ports in 2006. The House and Senate Armed Services Committee approved the authorization request for SLD; the House Energy and Water Appropriations Committee added $40 million, for a total of $123.9 million. For Megaports, the Senate Armed Services approved the Administration's request, the House added $15 million to the authorization request, and the Energy and Water Appropriations Committee added $60 million, for a total of $105.1 million. The appropriators noted that this added funding should be used to expand work at high-risk foreign ports. It reflects a growing concern in Congress with port security issues.

The FY2007 budget requested $119.3 million for the Second Line of Defense Program, with $72.5 million allocated to the Core program and $46.8 million allocated to Megaports. However, Congress appropriated $191.9 million in FY2007, with $116.1 million going to Megaports. In FY2008, Congress appropriated $266.9 million, with $136 million going to the core program and $130.8 million going to Megaports. These increases indicated that Congress has placed a high priority on detecting possible efforts to smuggle nuclear materials. In its request for FY2009, the Bush Administration sought $212 million for SLD, with $78.5 million going to the core program and $134 million going to Megaports. Congress appropriated $71.9 million for the core program and $102 million for Megaports.

The Obama Administration requested $78.4 million for the core program and $194 million for Megaports for FY2010; Congress appropriated this amount. The Administration requested $140.4 million for the core program in FY2011, and $124.9 million for Megaports. Congress authorized this amount in the FY2011 Defense Authorization Bill, but, with funding provided through the continuing resolution, the funding remained at $78.4 million for the core program and $194 million for Megaports. The Administration requested a total of $263.8 million for SLD in

---

[102] Hoehn, William. *Update on Legislation Affecting U.S-Former Soviet Union Nonproliferation and Threat Reduction.* RANSAC. November 17, 2003.

FY2012, with $129.4 allocated to the core program and $134.4 allocated to Megaports. Congress appropriated $262 million in FY2012, with a slight reduction taken from the Megaports portion.

In FY2013, the Obama Administration has requested only $92.6 million for the SLD program, with $73 million allocated to the core program and only $19.6 million allocated to Megaports. These reductions reflect the fact that DOE completed the installation of radiation detection equipment and Megaports equipment in FY2012, and will transition to sustainability programs in FY2013. According to DOE, it has, over the course of the program, installed radiation detection equipment at 450 sites in the former Soviet Union and Megaports equipment at 45 ports around the world.

Table 5, below, displays the funding history for many of these International Nuclear Materials and Cooperation programs. It aggregates the funding for the years between FY2002 and FY2006, then demonstrates how the budgets have evolved through the appropriations for FY2007-FY2013. The table demonstrates that funding for SLD, much of which is not spent in the former Soviet Union, increased sharply during the past decade. In addition, much of the funding in recent years has gone to programs to secure warheads and Navy and SRF sites and materials at Rosatom sites. As these programs wind down and wrap up, MPC&A funding, and DOE's contribution to cooperative nonproliferation programs in Russia, have begun to decline.

Table 5. Appropriations for M.C.&A and Related Programs

(in $ millions)

Program	FY2002-FY2005	FY2007	FY2008	FY2009	FY2010	FY2011	FY2012	FY2013 Request
Navy Complex	$212.6	$17.3	$13.2	$22.7	$33.9	$34.3	$33.6	$39.9
Strategic Rocket Forces	$206.2	$152.8	$121.9	$34.4	$48.6	$51.4	$59.1	$8.3
Rosatom (Minatom) Weapons Complex	$291.5	$94.0	$79.0	$56.1	$71.5	$93.3	$80.7	$47.0
Civilian Nuclear Sites	$128.8	$52.7	$54.2	$35.5	$63.5	$53	$59.1	$60.1
Material Consolidation and Conversion	$136.7	$23.8	$19.5	$21.6	$13.6	$13.9	$14.3	$17
National Programs and Sustainability	$206.8	$65.1	$69.6	$54.9	$68.5	$60.9	$60.9	$46.2
Second Line of Defense Core Program[a]	$151.2	$75.8	$136.0	$71.9	$78.4	$140.3	$129.4	$73.0
Total	$1,333.6	$481.5	$493.5	$297.1	$378	$447.1	437.1	291.5

Source: U.S. Department of Energy. FY2004, FY2005, FY2006, FY2007, FY2008, FY2009, FY2010, FY2011, FY2012, FY2013 Congressional Budget Requests. Detailed Budget Justifications.

a. This does not include funding for Megaports, which received $24 million in FY2004, $15 million in FY2005, $73.9 million in FY2006, $116.1 million in FY2007, $130.8 million in FY2008, $102.9 million in FY2009, $194 million in FY2010 and FY2011, and $134.4 in FY2012. The FY2013 request is $19.6 million.

Global Initiatives for Proliferation Prevention (Formerly Russian Transition Initiative)

In its budget request for FY2006, DOE renamed the Russian Transition Initiative, referring to it as the Global Initiatives for Proliferation Prevention. The program is now a part of the Global Security Engagement and Cooperation effort. The program also moved to the "Nonproliferation and International Security" portion of the DOE Nonproliferation budget. These changes reflect the fact that DOE can now spend funds from this program in nations outside the former Soviet Union, such as in Libya and Iraq.

The Russian Transition Initiative had combined two previous DOE programs, the Initiatives for Proliferation Prevention and the Nuclear Cities Initiative, that sought to stop the leakage of knowledge out of Russia's nuclear weapons complex to states or groups seeking their own nuclear weapons. According to DOE, these programs were designed to help Russia reduce the size of its nuclear weapons complex, by removing functions and equipment, and to create "sustainable non-weapons-related work" for scientists through technology projects that have "commercially-viable market opportunities."[103] The Bush Administration has stated that it hopes to expand the program from engaging only nuclear scientists to also engaging biological and chemical weapons scientists. It requested funding to expand the program to two chemical weapons institutes in FY2004.

Initiatives for Proliferation Prevention

The Initiatives for Proliferation Prevention (IPP) Program began in 1994. IPP has matched U.S. weapons labs and U.S. industry with Russian scientists and engineers in cooperative research projects with "high commercial potential." DOE claims that this focus on commercialization will help make the projects self-sustaining in the long term. The IPP program received $35 million in the FY1994 Foreign Operations Appropriations Act, before its funding moved to the Department of Energy. This initial funding helped establish nearly 200 research projects by 1995. Between FY1996 and FY2003, IAP received an additional $194 million. In FY2004, the Bush Administration requested around $23 million for projects funded through IPP, as a part of the overall request of $39.3 million for the Russian Transition Initiative. Congress approved this request.

The IPP program was the subject of review and criticism in a GAO study released in February 1999. The report noted that nearly half of the funds appropriated for the IAP program had been spent at the U.S. nuclear weapons labs and that, after subtracting the taxes, fees, and other charges removed by Russian officials, the Russian institutes had received only around one-third of the funds. The report also questioned DOE's oversight of the programs, noting that program officials did not always know how many scientists were receiving IAP funding. The report noted that the projects had not yet produced any commercial successes. DOE responded by stating that IAP had temporarily employed thousands of scientists in around 170 institutes. DOE also stated that the program did not subsidize scientists who were performing weapons-related work. Nevertheless, in FY2000, Congress reduced the Clinton Administration's request for funding for the IAP program from $30 million to $25 million and specified that no more than 35% of the funds be spent at the U.S. labs. It also mandated that the United States negotiate agreements with Russia to ensure that funds provided under this program are not subject to taxes in Russia. Furthermore, it requested that the Secretary of Energy review IAP programs for their commercialization potential.

---

[103] U.S. Department of Energy. FY2004 Congressional Budget Request. Detailed Budget Justifications. February 2003. p. 663.

The IPP Program was once again the subject of a critical GAO report in late 2007.[104] This report noted that DOE had overstated the number of scientists receiving support from this program by counting both weapons and non-weapons scientists in its totals. It also argues that DOE has overstated the number of long-term private sector jobs created as a result of this program, mostly because it does not have an independent way to confirm the reported number. Further, DOE does not have an exist strategy for the program, or a way to "graduate" institutes once they are self-sustaining or no longer pose a proliferation threat. This report has raised, anew, questions about the current value and future worthiness of the program.

DOE reports that the IPP program engaged 13,000 scientists, engineers, and technicians between FY1994 and FY2002, with 6,700 of them working on projects in 2002. At the end of 2002, IPP had 176 projects ongoing at 56 institutes in Russia, with 64 of these projects at facilities in the closed nuclear cities. IPP also had 14 projects at six institutes in Kazakhstan, and 13 projects at nine institutes in Ukraine. It has also been reported that 13 projects have become commercial ventures, and that the program has created 850 high tech jobs in Russia. Furthermore, the IPP program has received around $125 million in private sector matching funds.[105]

Nuclear Cities Initiative (NCI)

In August 1998, Vice President Gore and then-Prime Minister Carancha signed an agreement establishing the Nuclear Cities Initiative. This program is designed to bring commercial enterprises to Russia's closed nuclear cities, so that Russia can reduce the size of its weapons complex and so that the scientists and engineers will not be tempted to sell their knowledge to nations seeking nuclear weapons. The United States and Russia signed an implementing agreement in September 1998, and the program received its first funding of $15 million in FY1999. The NCI program received a total of nearly $87 million between FY1999 and FY2003; the Bush Administration has requested and received an additional $17 million for it within the funding for the Russian Transition Initiative.

Some Members of Congress and others, including GAO, also raised questions about the value and effectiveness of the NCI program. In its first budget for FY2002, the Bush Administration sought to reduce funding from $26 million in FY2001 to $6.6 million, limiting the program to 3 of Russia's 10 closed nuclear cities. It also indicated that it might seek to eliminate the program, merging its functions with the IAP program. Congress accepted this latter proposal, creating the Russian Transition Initiative, and it initially accepted the reduction in funding for the program. However, in the supplemental appropriations bill passed after the September 11 attacks, Congress added $15 million to the NCI program. Nevertheless, with limited funding and uncertain political support, the NCI program reportedly made limited progress in addressing the employment problems at Russia's closed nuclear cities. Some say that the merger with the IAP will bring stability and progress to the program's efforts. In late July 2003, the Bush Administration announced that the NCI program would cease to operate by the end of 2003. The United States and Russia were unable to agree on the liability provisions in an implementing agreement for the program. Ongoing projects continued through the end of 2003, but the program did not receive new funding or begin new projects.

---

[104] U.S. Government Accountability Office. DOE's Program to Assist Weapons Scientists in the Russia and Other Countries needs to be Reassessed. GAO-08-189, December 2007.

[105] *Controlling Nuclear Warheads and Materials: A Report Card and Action Plan*, by Matthew Bunn et al. Project on Managing the Atom. March 2003.

In its FY2005 budget request, the Administration allocated $41 million to the Russian Transition Initiative. Some of this funding supported ongoing NCI projects in Russia's closed nuclear cities. The Administration requested $37.9 million for its new Global Initiatives for Proliferation Prevention Program in FY2006. Congress authorized this amount in the FY2006 Defense Authorization Act and appropriated around $40 million in the Energy and Water Appropriations Act. Within this budget, the Administration planned to phase out the last of the NCI programs in Russia's closed city of Snezhinsk and to reduce its efforts in the closed city of Sarov. It would then focus funding on helping to redirect engineers and technicians associated with the shutdown of Russia's plutonium production reactors in Seversk and Zheleznogorsk (this program is described below). Hence, the budget reduction, when combined with the shifting of funds to nations outside the former Soviet Union, resulted in a contraction of efforts to redirect Russia's nuclear scientists and to reduce the size of Russia's nuclear weapons complex.

In the FY2007 budget request, these two programs moved again, to DOE's Nonproliferation and International Security account. The total request for both parts of the program equaled $28.1 million. DOE reported that the decline was due to reduced activity at two sites that were a part of NCI and to the deferral of work at two commercial sites. The House and Senate Armed Services Committees both approved the authorization request for these programs, but the Appropriations Committees increased the funding to $39.6 million. The FY2008 budget request sought $20.2 million for these programs. DOE has again indicated that the decline in funding reflects the termination of the NCI portion of the program. Congress appropriated $30.1 million. The FY2009 budget request included $23.8 million for these programs, but Congress appropriated only $15.4 million. The Obama Administration requested $20 million for these programs in FY2010; Congress appropriated $19.7 million. The Administration requested $18.4 million for FY2011 and $18.5 million in FY2012.

Elimination of Weapons-Grade Plutonium Production

In the early 1990s, the United States and Russia both pledged to end the production of plutonium for nuclear weapons. Russia, however, balked at suggestions that it shut its three remaining plutonium production reactors because it used the same reactors to produce light and heat in the cities of Tomsk and Krasnoyarsk. In an agreement signed in 1994, under the auspices of the high-level commission chaired by Vice President Gore and Russia's Prime Minister Chernomyrdin, the two sides agreed that they would work together to provide alternative energy sources for these Russian cities. This program began as a part of the DOD CTR program and moved to DOE in FY2002.

In the original 1994 agreement, Russia stated that it would shut the reactors by 2000, if the alternative energy facilities were developed in the same time frame. Initially, the two nations planned to replace the reactors with fossil-fueled power plants, but early studies concluded that the construction of these plants could cost up to $1 billion. Consequently, the two sides began to explore the possibility of converting the plutonium production reactors to a type whose spent fuel did not require reprocessing. These new reactors would no longer produce weapons-grade plutonium. Each side planned to pay half of the expected $160 million for this conversion project. However, over the next few years the expected cost of the core conversion more than doubled. After its financial crisis in 1998, Russia concluded that it could not pay its half. If the project had continued, the United States might have had to pay more than $300 million. At the same time, questions about the reactors' safety raised the possibility that they might need to be closed shortly after the core conversion was complete.

In late 1999, Minatom proposed that the two sides again pursue the replacement of the nuclear reactors with fossil fuel plants. After reducing the estimate for the necessary size of the plants, it estimated that the new project would cost about the same as the core conversion project. In late 2000 and early 2001, the two nations agreed to replace the reactors with fossil fuel plants. However, in FY2000 and FY2001, Congress prohibited the expenditure of any CTR funds for the construction of fossil fuel plants. When it completed its review of U.S. nonproliferation and threat reduction assistance to Russia, the Bush Administration endorsed the reactor shut-down program and transferred the effort from DOD to DOE.

DOD, DOE, and the State Department have all contributed to this project. The State Department contributed nearly $4.5 million in FY1995 and FY1999 to feasibility studies. DOD's budget included $10 million in FY1995 and $16 million in FY1996. It also included $32 million in FY2000, but these funds were rescinded after Congress prohibited their expenditure on fossil fuel plants. Congress transferred $32 million in FY2001 funds and $56 million in FY2002 funds from DOD to DOE, and appropriated $49 million in the DOE budget for FY2003. The Bush Administration requested and received $50 million for this effort in FY2004.[106] It requested a similar amount, $50.1 million, to continue this project in FY2005.

The United States and Russia concluded a new agreement to implement the reactor shutdown program in early 2003. According to NNSA, the new fossil fuel plants will be completed, and the old nuclear reactors shut down, in 2008 and 2011, assuming there are no further delays in the implementation of the agreement. The United States and Russia are also implementing efforts to improve safety at the reactors in the interim.[107] At the Seversk site, the program is shutting down two nuclear reactors and refurbishing an old fossil fuel plant from the 1950s. This project is slated to be completed by the end of December 2008. At Zheleznogorsk, the United States is not only helping Russia shut down the nuclear plant, but also helping it construct a new fossil fuel plant. According to DOE, this project is more than one-third complete, and should be done by 2011.

DOE requested $132 million for this program area in FY2006; this was a substantial increase over the $44 million appropriated in FY2005. DOE indicated that this request reflected its plans to expand significantly the construction activities associated with the fossil fuel plants at the Seversk site. In the FY2006 Defense Authorization Act (P.L. 109-163), Congress increased the funding for this project to over $200 million. Both the House and the Senate noted that they wanted to ensure that the shutdown of the Zheleznogorsk reactor remained on schedule. The Energy and Water Appropriations Act also increased funding for this program, but to only $176.2 million. The FY2007 budget requested $206.6 million for this program. The increase in funding is again directed at the Zheleznogorsk reactor, with the intent to complete the shutdown by 2010 instead of 2011. Congress appropriated $174.4 million. The FY2008 budget request sought $181.6 million for this project area. Within this request, funding for the Seversk site declined sharply, from $84.7 million to $19.4 million, as the project nears completion, and funding for the Zheleznogorsk site continues to rise, from $119.9 million to $160.8 million. The House Energy and Water Development Appropriations Committee added $10 million to this request to further accelerate work Zheleznogorsk. The Senate Appropriators, on the other hand, reduced the request, providing only $152.6 million. In the final budget, Zheleznogorsk received $159.1 million, and

---

[106] *Controlling Nuclear Warheads and Materials: A Report Card and Action Plan*, by Matthew Bunn et al. Project on Managing the Atom. March 2003.

[107] For details on components of the reactor shut-down program, see U.S. Department of Energy. *FY2004 Congressional Budget Request*. Detailed Budget Justifications. February 2003. p. 722-726.

---

the total project area $179.9 million. DOE requested $141.3 million for FY2009. There is no funding for Seversk, and Zheleznogorsk would receive $139.3 million. The remaining $2 million is allocated to crosscutting and technical support activities.

The Obama Administration requested only $24.5 million for this project in FY2010, and this was expected to be the last year of funding for this program, as the work at Zheleznogorsk was almost complete. Congress authorized and appropriated this amount for FY2010. There was no funding requested for this project in FY2011, FY2012, and FY2013.

Fissile Materials Disposition

In September 1998, the United States and Russia agreed to convert surplus weapons-grade plutonium to a form that could not be returned to nuclear weapons. In the Plutonium Management and Disposition Agreement, signed in September 2000, each side agreed to dispose of 34 metric tons of weapons-grade plutonium, and to do so at roughly the same time. This agreement was designed to ease concerns about the possible theft or diversion of weapons-grade plutonium by nations or others seeking to develop their own nuclear weapons.

According to the agreement, the parties could use two methods for disposing of the plutonium—they could either convert it to mixed oxide fuel (MOX) for nuclear power reactors or immobilize it and dispose of it in a way that would preclude its use in nuclear weapons. Some analysts have criticized the MOX option on the principle of opposing any use of plutonium in power generation. From this point of view, nations that do not possess nuclear weapons could use a plutonium-base power fuel cycle as a cover for developing nuclear weapons. If weapons states such as Russia and the United States used plutonium for power generation, according to this argument, it would be more difficult to persuade non-weapons states not to do so. However, Russia has expressed little interest in the permanent disposal of plutonium, noting that the material could have great value for its civilian power program. The United States initially intended to pursue both options. However, after reviewing U.S. nonproliferation policies in 2001, the Bush Administration concluded that this approach would be too costly. Instead, it outlined a plan for the United States to convert almost all its surplus plutonium to MOX fuel. Congress appropriated $152 million for FY2003 to begin construction of three facilities in Savannah River, SC, to pursue the MOX option, and the FY2004 request included $416 million for construction and $194 million for operation and maintenance for the U.S. surplus plutonium disposal program. The FY2005 budget request reduced funding for the U.S. program by about $50 million.

The United States and international community agreed to pay a large portion of the cost for Russia's plutonium disposition program. According to the State Department, U.S. allies, including Great Britain, France, and Japan, pledged to provide $700 million.[108] Congress appropriated $200 million for this program for FY1999, but most of these funds have not been spent. The Bush Administration's FY2004 budget justification requested $47 million for Russian Fissile Materials Disposition "Operations and Maintenance," and prior balances totaling $151 million will be spent in the Russian Federation "in accordance with a new detailed program execution plan to be provided to Congress."[109]

---

[108] U.S. Department of State. *Fiscal Year 2002 Performance and Accountability Report*. p. 62.

[109] U.S. Department of Energy. *FY2004 Congressional Budget Request*. Detailed Budget Justifications. DOE/ME-0016. February 2003. Vol. 1, p. 548.

However, in late July 2003, the Bush Administration announced that the plutonium disposition program would not pursue additional contracts in 2004 because the United States and Russia were unable to agree on the liability provisions for a new implementing agreement for the program. The two nations reportedly reached a liability agreement in 2005, although it has not yet been signed by Russia's President Putin. The FY2005 budget included $64 million for U.S. assistance to Russia on plutonium disposition, under the assumption that the nations would resolve their differences and the program would resume. Congress authorized and appropriated the requested amount for FY2005 but questioned the Administration's ability to begin construction in May 2005, an event which eventually did not occur. The Administration requested an additional $64 million for this program in FY2006, but Congress appropriated only $34 million, again questioning the timing for the start of the project.

The Administration requested $34.7 million for FY2007 for this project. Both the House and the Senate Armed Services Committees have expressed wide-ranging and deep concerns about this program. In particular, Russia has indicated that it may not pursue the MOX program to eliminate its plutonium, opting instead for the construction of fast breeder reactors that could burn plutonium directly for energy production. The United States might not fund this effort, as many in the United States argue that breeder reactors, which produce more plutonium than they consume, would undermine nonproliferation objectives. As a result of these concerns, the House Armed Services Committee deleted all funding for this program in Russia in the FY2007 Defense Authorization Bill. The Senate Armed Services provided the funding, but fenced it pending a report from the Secretary of Energy; the conference committee adopted this approach. Congress has also questioned the value of continuing with the U.S. MOX program and has reduced funding for this effort as well.

The Bush Administration did not request any additional funding for this program area in FY2008. In late November 2007, the United States and Russia announced that they had reached agreement of how they would proceed with this program.[110] Generally, the United States has agreed that Russia can burn some of the plutonium in breeder reactors but that the reactors will be modified so that they will not produce more plutonium than they burn. At the same time, the United States will continue to fund construction of the MOX fuel plant, and Russia will convert some of its plutonium into this fuel. The Bush Administration hailed this agreement as providing a way forward to dispose of plutonium; critics have complained that the agreement will sharply slow the process of eliminating Russia's weapons-grade plutonium. This agreement came too late, however, to change the funding profile for FY2008 and the Omnibus Appropriations Bill did not contain any funding for this program area. The Bush Administration indicated that funding from prior years remains available to support this program. It requested only $1 million for FY2009 to support technical oversight of the program by the U.S. nuclear weapons laboratories.

The Obama Administration also requested, and Congress appropriated, only $1 million for this program in FY2010. However, the Administration requested $113 million for Russian Materials Disposition in FY2011. In the budget request, the Administration indicated that it believes the Protocol that contains the agreement negotiated in 2007 would be signed in early 2010, which will allow the United States to begin to fund its portion of Russia's materials disposition effort. Congress authorized funding for this program in the FY2011 Defense Authorization Act, but it did not appropriate funding in the continuing resolution because the program had not received

---

[110] Springer, Sebastian. U.S., Russia Agree on Way Ahead for Plutonium Disposition. Inside Defense. Tuesday, November 20, 2007.

any funds in FY2010. Moreover, the Administration withdrew the request for $100 million of the FY2010 funds, during the debates over the continuing resolutions. It requested $31 million for this program in FY2012, but indicated, in the budget documents, that it expected to use some of the funds from the FY2011 request in FY2012. Congress appropriated only $1 million for Russian fissile materials disposition in FY2012, and the Administration has requested only $3.8 million for FY2013.

Issues for Congress

Congress has addressed a number of issues during the years since it passed the Nunn-Lugar amendment and DOD established the Cooperative Threat Reduction Program. Many of these are discussed in detail in CRS Report 97-1027, *Nunn-Lugar Cooperative Threat Reduction Programs: Issues for Congress*. Some of these issues have grown out of concerns with specific projects, as has been the case with the dispute over the chemical weapons destruction facility at Shchuch'ye. Others have derived from broader concerns about whether threat reduction assistance to Russia and the other former Soviet states serves broader U.S. national security goals. The question of whether U.S. threat reduction and nonproliferation assistance represents "defense by other means"—as former Secretary of Defense William Perry used to argue—or foreign aid— as some in Congress often assert—continues to echo in debates about these programs. Some program critics and some Members of Congress also continue to question whether U.S. assistance allows Russia to divert its own resources to the development and production of new weapons that could threaten the United States. Secretary of Defense Rumsfeld raised this question during his nomination hearing in January 2001.

On the other hand, as U.S. threat reduction and nonproliferation assistance to Russia moves through its second decade, many of the issues discussed during the debates over the programs reflect new concerns raised during assessments of how the programs performed in their first decade and how they might improve in the second. Many of these issues also reflect the growing focus of the programs on the potential link between weapons of mass destruction that might leak out of Russia and terrorist organizations that might seek these weapons to attack the United States and its allies. The discussion below reviews many of these issues, describing concerns raised by those who support and those who criticize the programs. The discussion draws heavily on the findings and proposals outlined by several non-governmental reports on U.S. threat reduction and nonproliferation assistance. These provide a more detailed description of the status of the programs and proposals for the future.[111]

---

[111] See, for example, *Reshaping U.S.-Russian Threat Reduction: New Approaches for the Second Decade*. Carnegie Endowment for International Peace and Russian American Nuclear Security Advisory Council. November 2002. http://www.carnegieendowment.org/publications/index.cfm?fa=view&id=1117&prog=zgp&proj=znpp; U.S. Department of Energy. The Secretary of Energy Advisory Board. *A Report Card on the Department of Energy's Nonproliferation Programs With Russia*. Howard Baker and Lloyd Cutler. Russia Task Force. January 10, 2001. http://www.seab.energy.gov/publications/rusrpt.pdf; *Controlling Nuclear Warheads and Materials: A Report Card and Action Plan*, by Matthew Bunn et al. Project on Managing the Atom. March 2003, http://www nti.org/e_research/ cnwm/cnwm.pdf, and Einhorn, Robert J. and Michelle A. Flournoy, *Protecting Against the Spread of Nuclear, Biological, and Chemical Weapons. An Action Agenda for Global Partnership*. CSIS Report. January 2003. http://www.sgpproject.org/publications/publications_index html. *Global Security Engagement: A New Model for Cooperative Threat Reduction*. National Academy of Sciences. April 2009.

Organization and Coordination

As was noted above, CTR implementation was slow during the program's early years. The need to negotiate umbrella agreements with Russia, and to establish a "culture of cooperation," was a key reason for the early delays. But some analysts also cite the need to coordinate project planning among several U.S government agencies as a problem. Many analysts contend that coordination problems remain today, even though each of the three key agencies—DOD, DOE and State—funds and manages its own projects. These agencies still need to coordinate their efforts to avoid duplication and, in some cases, to share resources and expertise. In addition, with the programs spread among three agencies, no one in the U.S. government has taken the lead in setting policies and priorities for U.S. threat reduction and nonproliferation assistance, or in serving as an advocate for these programs in interagency debates. Some Members of Congress and analysts outside government have proposed two specific solutions that they believe will improve implementation of U.S. threat reduction and nonproliferation assistance—the creation of a strategic plan and the designation of an overall program coordinator.

Strategic Plan

Many analysts, both inside and outside the U.S. government, believe that U.S. threat reduction and nonproliferation programs would benefit from the development of a government-wide strategic plan. Some officials and analysts expected the Bush Administration to develop a more comprehensive strategic plan for these programs during its review of U.S. nonproliferation assistance to Russia in 2001.[112] That review just identified those programs that would receive greater resources and expanded mandates. But, according to former Senator Pete Domenici, "these programs frequently are intertwined and interrelated in various complex and difficult ways."[113] According to one analyst who has participated in both DOD and DOE programs, the growth in U.S. programs "has been by and large, organic, with each agency pursuing its own contacts and relationships in recipient countries, assembling and justifying its own budget, implementing programs based on its own culture and approaches, and interacting with its own Congressional oversight committees."[114] Most analysts agree that a comprehensive strategic plan would allow for the development of an overall set of goals for U.S. assistance, better coordination among programs, a more consistent method to set priorities and measure progress, and a coordinated way to determine when and how the United States had achieved its goals and could complete a program.

---

[112] "I would hope that the real result of the review would lead to a more comprehensive approach, a more integrated approach, to nonproliferation and threat reduction, so that the individual program can be seen and measured in light of an overall approach and clear goals, and so the individual programs can support each other more synergistically." U.S. House. Committee on Armed Services. Hearing. Department of Energy Budget Request for FY2002. p. 9. Statement of Gen. John A. Gordon, Administrator, National Nuclear Security Administration. June 27, 2001.

[113] U.S. Senate. Committee on Governmental Affairs, Subcommittee on International Security, Proliferation and Federal Services. Hearing. *Combating Proliferation of Weapons of Mass Destruction (WMD) with Non-proliferation Programs: Non-proliferation Assistance Coordination Act of 2001.* November 14, 2001.

[114] Ibid. Statement of Laura Holgate, Vice President of the Russian Newly Independent States Program, Nuclear Threat Initiative.

Program Coordination

Many analysts have also called for the creation of a high-level program coordinator or a high-level interagency committee chaired by a representative of the National Security Council. This program coordinator would set a consistent direction by setting priorities, resolving competing demands for budgetary resources, eliminating overlap and redundancy, and coordinating implementation across agencies. This individual would also raise the political profile of the programs, bringing consistent political leadership that many analysts believe is lacking. They argue that continued, coordinated success for the programs requires "active political engagement at the White House, cabinet, and sub-cabinet political appointee levels in the U.S. government."[115]

Neither the Clinton nor the Bush Administrations accepted proposals for a single, high-level program coordinator, arguing that interagency coordination already occurs. According to an official from the Bush Administration, "U.S. policy implementation and oversight of nonproliferation assistance to the states of the former Soviet Union is coordinated at senior levels by the Proliferation Strategy Policy Coordinating Committee, or PCC, chaired by a National Security Council senior director, with assistant secretary-level representatives from State, Defense, Energy and other concerned agencies."[116] Others have argued that a new interagency committee would complicate the existing interagency coordinating process.[117]

Congress, however, continued to support a high-level coordinator, or czar, for the threat reduction and nonproliferation programs. In late 2006, Representative Ellen Tauscher and Senator Hillary Rodham Clinton introduced legislation, known as the Nuclear Terrorism Prevention Act of 2006 (H.R. 6419, S. 4103), that would have created a Senior Advisor to the President for the prevention of nuclear terrorism. This advisor would have, among other things, been responsible for "overseeing the development, by the relevant Federal departments and agencies, of accelerated and strengthened program implementation strategies and diplomatic strategies ... and overseeing the development of budget requests for these programs and ensuring that they adequately reflect the priority of the problem." The first piece of legislation introduced in the 110th Congress, the Implementing the 9/11 Commission Recommendations Act of 2007 (H.R. 1, S. 4) took up the same theme. It established an Office of the United States Coordinator for the Prevention of Weapons of Mass Destruction Proliferation and Terrorism within the Executive Office of the President. This advisor would, among other things, lead inter-agency coordination of U.S. efforts to implement its WMD nonproliferation strategy and would oversee "the development of a comprehensive and coordinated budget for programs and initiatives to prevent WMD proliferation and terrorism, ensuring that such budget adequately reflects the priority of the challenges and is effectively executed, and carrying out other appropriate budgetary authorities."

The Bush Administration never filled this position with a designated Director on the NSC staff, and indicated that the existing NSC staff could achieve the goals outlined in the legislation. The Obama Administration, in contrast, has created and filled a new NSC position for the coordinator

---

[115] *Options for Increased U.S. Russian Nuclear Nonproliferation Cooperation and Projected Costs.* RANSAC, October 2001.

[116] U.S. Senate. Committee on Governmental Affairs, Subcommittee on International Security, Proliferation and Federal Services. Hearing. *Combating Proliferation of Weapons of Mass Destruction (WMD) with Non-proliferation Programs: Non-proliferation Assistance Coordination Act of 2001.* Statement of Vann Van Diepen, Deputy Assistant Secretary of State for Nonproliferation. November 29, 2001.

[117] Ibid. Statement of Marshall Billingslea, Deputy Assistant Secretary of Defense for Negotiations.

of the prevention of WMD proliferation and terrorism. This NSC director reportedly has a deputy director who will focus specifically on threat reduction efforts, and will seek to coordinate the threat reduction and nonproliferation programs in DOE, DOD, and the State Department.

Most analysts agree that the budget responsibility addressed in this legislation would be critical to the success of this new policy position. A White House-based nonproliferation "czar" may be able to communicate high-level interest and political commitment to the programs. However, unless this individual could control the budgets of the programs involved to ensure that funding levels matched stated priorities, and unless the individual could implement corrective actions to ensure that programs achieved their objectives, it seems unlikely that he or she would be able to establish priorities and enforce them across government agencies. A high-level committee might have greater success creating a consensus about priorities, because each agency would have a representative at the table. But it might still find it difficult to match funding levels to these priorities because each agency's budget would still reflect the overall priorities and missions of the agency.

Access and Transparency

Many analysts and government officials note that the primary barrier to successful implementation of many threat reduction projects has been the need to gain access and transparency from officials in the recipient nations, particularly Russia. As was noted above, Russia was slow to provide the United States with access to nuclear weapons storage areas, which delayed the implementation of security improvements at these facilities. It has not provided complete information about or access to facilities in its biological weapons complex, and, in spite of more than eight years of negotiations, the United States and Russia still have not completed a transparency agreement for the facility in Mayak that will store fissile materials removed from weapons. Furthermore, Russia has not provided the United States with access to many facilities in Russia's nuclear weapons complex, leaving large holes in the U.S. ability to improve security for the nuclear materials at those facilities.

Although many analysts note that Russia's interest in protecting secret details about its nuclear weapons programs is understandable, most also argue that this secrecy, and the resulting delays in program implementation, serve to undermine support in the United States for threat reduction and nonproliferation programs. While most agree that Russia must step forward to solve this problem,[118] they also note that the United States does not have a "systematic approach to identifying and addressing these problems."[119] Each agency has developed its own solutions. For example, in some cases, DOE has used photographs and diagrams, instead of on-site visits, to identify security weaknesses and design security improvements at nuclear complex sites. Analysts have identified this "ad hoc" process as one further incentive for better coordination among threat

---

[118] The Baker-Cutler report notes that Russian official point out that "transparency and access matters are far from routine in Russian bureaucracy." Russia does not have procedures for foreigners to have routine access to facilities in the nuclear weapons complex, so requests are treated on a case-by-case basis. They need a high-level government decision to lead to routine access, rather than having it treated on a case-by-case basis. U.S. Department of Energy. The Secretary of Energy Advisory Board. *A Report Card on the Department of Energy's Nonproliferation Programs With Russia.* Howard Baker and Lloyd Cutler. Russia Task Force. January 10, 2001. p. 22.

[119] *Reshaping U.S.-Russian Threat Reduction: New Approaches for the Second Decade.* Carnegie Endowment for International Peace and Russian American Nuclear Security Advisory Council. November 2002. p. 4.

---

reduction programs; a single program coordinator could help agencies identify problems and share solutions.

In the FY2006 Defense Authorization Act (P.L. 109-163), Congress called on the Administration to submit a report on the impediments to successful implementation of these programs. The report is to both identify these impediments and outline U.S. plans to overcome them. Problems with access to Russian facilities is one of the impediments cited in the reporting requirement.

Liability Protections and the Umbrella Agreement

In 1992, the United States and Russia signed an umbrella agreement that outlined the rights and responsibilities assumed by each of the parties when implementing programs funded by U.S. threat reduction assistance. This agreement provides the legal framework that allows for program implementation; if it were to lapse, the United States could not award any new contracts for projects funded by U.S. assistance. The original agreement was set to last for seven years; the two parties agreed to extend it for another seven years in 1999. It was again set to expire in June 2006. At the time it was signed, this agreement applied only to those programs funded by the Department of Defense, but the Department of Energy has adopted a similar agreement to cover many of its programs in the former Soviet Union.

The most contentious elements of the umbrella agreement are the provisions that cover liability for accidents or incidents that might occur during project implementation. In the original agreement, Russia assumed all liability, freeing U.S. contractors from the threat of legal action or the possible need to pay fines and penalties if accidents were to occur. However, in recent years, Russia has objected to these blanket liability provisions, arguing, at a minimum, that U.S. contractors should be held liable for accidents resulting from sabotage. As was noted above, this disagreement impeded the conclusion of a new implementation agreement for DOE's Plutonium Disposition Program. When resolving this dispute, the United States was reluctant to ease its stand that U.S. contractors receive blanket liability protection, in part, because it was afraid that this would set an unacceptable precedent during negotiations on the broader umbrella agreement.

However, by the middle of 2005, the United States and Russia both recognized that a failure to resolve the liability debate stalling the Plutonium Disposition Program could, eventually, lead to a failure to resolve the dispute in negotiations over the umbrella agreement. This, in turn, could stall or stop a nonproliferation program that most experts agreed had made great strides to secure weapons and materials in Russia. Conversely, if the two states could find an acceptable solution for the DOE program's agreement, it might ease efforts to conclude a new umbrella agreement. During this process, contractors participating in the DOE program reportedly noted that they would not object to a provision that placed liability for accidents resulting from sabotage onto the U.S. companies; they noted that this could expose them to Russia's legal system, but they also noted that the United States might address this through a separate international treaty or by focusing on Russian liability law, rather than by pressing for blanket liability protection.[120]

The two sides reached agreement on the liability provisions for the DOE programs during the G-8 summit at Gleneagles, Scotland, in July 2005. Reports indicate that, in exchange for the U.S.

---

[120] Fiorill, Joe. Hopes, Pressure Rise for End to U.S.-Russian Stalemate on Liability in Nuclear Security Projects. Global Security Newswire. July 1, 2005.

giving up its insistence on blanket liability protection in future contracts, the two countries would set up a separate process for addressing any situations that might arise as a result of sabotage.[121]

In mid-June 2006, the United States and Russia reached agreement on liability protections and extended the umbrella agreement for another seven years.[122] This concluded the agreement just days before the existing agreement was due to expire. Reports indicate that the new agreement retains the original agreement's blanket liability protections for existing projects but will address Russia's concerns when implementing future projects. Hence, U.S. contractors could be liable for damages caused by sabotage or other accidents, in some circumstances.

Certifications and Waivers

The original Nunn-Lugar amendment contained six "exclusions" that set out conditions the recipients had to meet before receiving U.S. threat reduction assistance. The United States could not provide assistance until the President certified to Congress that each recipient nation was "committed to:"

> (1) making a substantial investment of its resources for dismantling or destroying such weapons;
>
> (2) forgoing any military modernization program that exceeds legitimate defense requirements and forgoing the replacement of destroyed weapons of mass destruction;
>
> (3) forgoing any use of fissionable and other components of destroyed nuclear weapons in new nuclear weapons;
>
> (4) facilitating United States verification of weapons destruction carried out under section 212;
>
> (5) complying with all relevant arms control agreements; and
>
> (6) observing internationally recognized human rights, including the protection of minorities."[123]

Congress expected the President to exercise his judgment when deciding whether to issue the certifications. For example, the legislation states that the recipient nations must be "committed to" the policies listed in the six exclusions, a standard which can be less demanding than one that requires precise behavior. The Clinton Administration certified Russia for several years, even though the United States had questions about Russia's compliance with chemical and biological weapons agreements, because Russia's President Yeltsin had offered verbal assurances of his commitment to resolve the outstanding questions. Using the same information, the Bush Administration withheld Russia's certification. In addition, the exclusions do not define many of their terms. For example, they state that a recipient must make "a substantial investment" of its own resources, but it does not define a level of investment that would be necessary. They also state that the recipients must forgo military modernization programs that exceed legitimate

---

[121] Liabilities Deal Rests With Russian Prime Minister for Final Approval. Inside the Pentagon. December 22, 2005.

[122] The White House. Office of the Press Secretary. Cooperative Threat Reduction Agreement with Russia Extended. June 19, 2006.

[123] P.L. 102-228, Sec 211, paragraph (b).

defense requirements, but it does not ban all military modernization or indicate how much would be too much.

Congress debated adding new or modified exclusions to the CTR legislation several times over the life of the CTR program. In some years, some Members have sought to provide more precise standards of behavior for the recipient nations; in others, they have sought to add new requirements linking receipt of assistance to a greater number of policy areas. Congress has rejected many of these efforts, particularly if they appeared certain to cut off U.S. threat reduction assistance to Russia. Instead, it has usually crafted requirements with language that provides the President with the flexibility to balance U.S. concerns about the recipients' policies against the U.S. interest in continuing efforts to contain and eliminate weapons of mass destruction.[124]

Congress did add new certification requirements related to the construction of the chemical weapons destruction facility at Shchuch'ye in FY1998 and FY1999. These stated that "no funds authorized to be appropriated under this or any other Act for FY1998 for Cooperative Threat Reduction programs may be obligated or expended for chemical weapons destruction activities ... until the President submits to Congress a written certification" that:

> (A) Russia is making reasonable progress toward the implementation of the Bilateral Destruction Agreement;
>
> (B) the United States and Russia have made substantial progress toward the resolution, to the satisfaction of the United States, of outstanding compliance issues under the Wyoming Memorandum of Understanding and the Bilateral Destruction Agreement; and
>
> (C) Russia has fully and accurately declared all information regarding its unitary and binary chemical weapons, chemical weapons facilities, and other facilities associated with chemical weapons.

However, Congress permitted the President to submit an alternative certification, which stated that "the national security interests of the United States could be undermined by a United States policy not to carry out chemical weapons destruction activities under the Cooperative Threat Reduction programs." But when Congress resumed funding for Shchuch'ye in FY2002, after a two year prohibition, it restored the certification requirements without the alternative provision. The United States could not provide funding for chemical weapons destruction activities in Russia until the Secretary of Defense certified that there has been:

> (1) information provided by Russia, that the United States assesses to be full and accurate, regarding the size of the chemical weapons stockpile of Russia;
>
> (2) a demonstrated annual commitment by Russia to allocate at least $25,000,000 to chemical weapons elimination;
>
> (3) development by Russia of a practical plan for destroying its stockpile of nerve agents;
>
> (4) enactment of a law by Russia that provides for the elimination of all nerve agents at a single site;

---

[124] For a detailed review of the history of the CTR certification requirements, see CRS Memorandum for Congress. *Certification Requirements Affecting the Nunn-Lugar Cooperative Threat Reduction Program.* By Amy F. Woolf. December 23, 2002.

(5) an agreement by Russia to destroy or convert its chemical weapons production facilities at Volgograd and Novocheboksark; and

(6) a demonstrated commitment from the international community to fund and build infrastructure needed to support and operate the facility.

The Bush Administration announced, in April 2002, that it could not certify that Russia was committed to its arms control obligations under the Chemical Weapons and Biological Weapons Conventions. This decision stalled many ongoing CTR projects by precluding the signing and implementation of new contracts. Furthermore, in an effort to balance its stated support for CTR with this decision, the Administration asked Congress to provide it with the authority to waive the certification requirements so that it could continue to fund CTR programs in Russia. Most Members of Congress agreed with the Administration's view that the CTR programs continued to serve U.S. national security interests, and the House and Senate each included a waiver authority in its version of the Defense Authorization Bill. The Senate provided the President with permanent waiver authority; once passed, the authority would remain available to the President in all future fiscal years. The House sought a less generous provision, providing the President with the authority to waive the certification requirements only in FY2003. The conference committee, in Section 1306 (H.Rept. 107-436), provided the President with the authority to waive the certification requirements for three years. But this waiver only applied to the original six exclusions, not the separate certification for Shchuch'ye. Congress included one year of waiver authority for that project in the FY2003 Defense Appropriations Bill (P.L. 107-248), the FY2004 Defense Authorization Bill (P.L. 108-136), and the FY2005 Defense Authorization Bill (P.L. 108-375).

The three years of waiver authority in the FY2003 Defense Authorization Act expired at the end of FY2005. The House, in its version of the FY2006 Defense Authorization Bill provided the President with another three years of waiver authority. The Senate, in contrast, provided the President with unlimited waiver authority. The conference committee adopted the Senate position. The President must still present a waiver each year, if he cannot certify Russia's compliance with the requirements, but this authority is available to him every year. In its version of the FY2007 Defense Authorization Bill, the Senate approved language that would have eliminated the certification requirements from the CTR legislation. The House rejected this approach, although the final version of the bill continues to provide the President with unlimited waver authority.

The Bush Administration indicated that it believed that the combination of certification requirements and Presidential waivers was an essential part of its effort to use the CTR program to encourage greater openness in Russia and to transform Russian behavior. They allow the United States to signal to Russia that it will hold it to a high standard, and, although the President can waive the certifications, he does not have to if Russian behavior does not meet U.S. standards. Some in Congress supported this approach. They agreed that the CTR program should be afforded a high priority, but they noted that it could not proceed in a vacuum, without consideration for Russian behavior in other policy areas.

Some, however, disagreed with this approach. They believed that U.S. threat reduction assistance to Russia should be of the highest priority, and although Russian policies in other areas are important, they should not interfere with the elimination and containment of weapons of mass destruction. Some of these Members proposed that Congress amend the CTR legislation to remove the certification requirements altogether. Others believed that Congress should provide the President with permanent waiver authority so that this debate does not stop the program, as it did in 2002, again in the future.

Some in Congress, however, believe that Russian policies in other areas—such as Russian nuclear cooperation with Iran, Russian military modernization, and the lack of Russian compliance with arms control—can create new threats to U.S. security and, therefore, are of higher priority than threat reduction assistance. They argued that the President should have only a limited ability to waive the certification requirements.

The 110th Congress addressed this issue again; both the House and Senate versions of the Defense Authorization Bill would eliminate the certification requirements from the CTR program. The conference report accepted this provision, and, as a result, U.S. assistance under the CTR program is no longer subject to the certification requirements that have been the cause of so much debate.

Funding and Focus of the Programs

Funding

The United States currently allocates slightly more than $1 billion per year to its threat reduction and nonproliferation programs in the former Soviet Union; it spends and additional several hundred million dollars on these types of programs in nations outside the former Soviet Union. These programs expanded sharply in the latter half of the 1990s. Yet many analysts have argued that the United States should commit a far greater sum to these efforts. The Baker-Cutler report, for example, released in January 2001, argued that the United States should spend up to $30 billion over the next 10 years on DOE's programs to secure nuclear materials.[125] This amount did not include funding for DOD or State Department programs, which could total around $5 billion over 10 years if spending continues at the current level.

Most analysts agree that added funding will not necessarily accelerate all U.S. programs. They acknowledge that implementation problems, such as the absence of access to many facilities and the U.S. failure to certify Russia for receipt of CTR assistance for most of 2002, slowed progress and left significant amounts of money unspent. On the other hand, they have identified numerous programs that might achieve greater results with increased funding. These include the science centers in Moscow and Kiev, where the United States and its partners have had to limit the number of scientists who receive research grants because of limits on the available funds. This list at one time also included the program to dispose of plutonium in Russia, where added funding might have sped construction of the MOX facility and hasten the elimination of weapons grade plutonium, and the program to eliminate Russia's plutonium producing reactors, where greater funding is now leading to the completion of replacement energy plants. Export and border control programs might also accelerate their progress with added funding, leading to the installation of improved equipment and procedures at a greater number of border crossing points.

The Bush Administration generally agreed with the need to add funding to some programs to accelerate their progress, and it took this route with several programs, such as the science centers and export and border control programs, during its first term. It also called for added international funding to help accelerate the shutdown of Russia's plutonium-producing reactors and to speed

---

[125] U.S. Department of Energy. The Secretary of Energy Advisory Board. *A Report Card on the Department of Energy's Nonproliferation Programs With Russia.* Howard Baker and Lloyd Cutler. Russia Task Force. January 10, 2001. p. 20.

security improvements at storage sites for Russian nuclear warheads. However, analysts note that, with a fixed budget of around $1 billion per year, the United States will be able to expand these programs and introduce new programs only if it reduces funding for other programs. But other programs, such as the effort to help Russia dispose of its weapons-grade plutonium, could consume rapidly increasing sums in the future. Consequently, a fixed budget could force trade-offs between projects. For example, in its budget request for FY2004, DOE sought to add funding to accelerate the blend-down of highly enriched uranium and to fund the new program to identify and secure radiological sources. At the same time, it has reduced funding for MPC&A projects in Russia's nuclear weapons complex.

On the other hand, some current programs are beginning to finish their missions, allowing increased funding for other programs. Many of the capital-intensive construction projects funded during the 1990s fall into this category, as is evidenced by the reduced budgets for strategic offensive arms elimination and the construction of the chemical weapons destruction facility. Some have even noted that, as these large projects conclude, the United States might find it difficult to fulfill its commitment to spend $1 billion each year. DOD's CTR budget has already declined, and funding in DOE's budget for programs in Russia declined as it completed many of the security upgrades at nuclear weapons storage facilities. These changes could pave the way for added funding for new projects in the former Soviet Union, or they could release funds for use on other projects with an anti-terrorism focus, possibly outside the former Soviet Union. If recent trends continue, however, it seems quite likely that, while the U.S. budget for nonproliferation and threat reduction assistance may hold steady, or even increase a little, funding for programs in the former Soviet Union could decline in the near future.

Moreover, President Obama has pledged to secure all vulnerable nuclear materials around the world in four years and the Administration held a nuclear security summit in April 2010. Most analysts agree that this endeavor could require significant increases in funds for some threat reduction and nonproliferation programs outside the former Soviet Union. It is not yet clear whether these increases will come from a new, larger budget, from funds made available after the conclusion of some ongoing projects, or from a reduction in funding for some ongoing projects in the former Soviet Union.

Focus

U.S. threat reduction and nonproliferation programs have pursued a number of different types of projects, trying different solutions to different problems. However, most have followed one theme—these projects have sought to consolidate, contain, and destroy weapons and materials, and to consolidate and contain weapons knowledge, so that they would not leak out of the former Soviet Union. In essence, the United States has sought to identify materials and knowledge that might leak out of Russia and to contain them at their source. Several of the new projects initiated recently, such as the WMD Proliferation Prevention Project at DOD and DOE Second Line of Defense, take a different approach. Instead of improving security at the source, they seek set up barriers outside the nuclear weapons complex to prevent these resources from leaving the territory of the former Soviet Union.

These two approaches can be complementary and provide a "layered defense" against the leakage of weapons, materials, and knowhow. However, in an era of constrained budgets, they might also compete for funding and political support. Furthermore, many analysts believe that the most effective approach to keeping nuclear materials away from terrorists is to protect them at their source, at facilities in Russia's nuclear complex.[126] Consequently, Congress may address the issue of focus and priorities in its debate over U.S. threat reduction and nonproliferation assistance.

Globalization and International Cooperation

There is near-universal agreement, both within the U.S. government and among analysts outside the U.S. government, that the potential proliferation of weapons of mass destruction to rogue nations or terrorist groups presents a global problem that requires an international response. While the legacy of the Soviet Union's weapons programs may create the most immediate and largest threat, other nations also possess materials, weapons, or knowledge that could leak out beyond their borders to those seeking their own nuclear, chemical or biological weapons.[127] In addition, although the United States has spent more than 15 years trying to help Russia and the other former Soviet states secure their weapons, materials, and knowledge, other nations can contribute to this effort with funding and cooperative programs. The following section addresses three characteristics of the proposals for the "globalization" of threat reduction and nonproliferation assistance. The first, the G-8 Global Partnership Against the Spread of Weapons and Materials of Mass Destruction, is an initiative that has expanded the list of countries contributing to threat reduction and nonproliferation programs in Russia. The second describes possible initiatives to extend U.S. threat reduction assistance to nations outside the former Soviet Union. The third is a more general approach to encourage all nations to better account for and secure their weapons of mass destruction and materials that might become attractive targets for terrorists seeking their own weapons of mass destruction.

The G-8 Global Partnership

During the G-8 summit in Kananaskis, Canada, in July 2002, the United States, Russia, and other G-8 leaders agreed to establish a long-term program—the G-8 Global Partnership Against Weapons of Mass Destruction—to stop the spread of weapons of mass destruction and related materials and technology. Under this program, known as 10+10 over 10, the United States has pledged to provide $10 billion over 10 years to sustain ongoing threat reduction programs in Russia; this amount of $1 billion per year is equal to current U.S. spending on threat reduction and nonproliferation programs in Russia, so the U.S. commitment would not necessarily signal an increase in the U.S. level of effort. The other G-7 nations have also agreed that they will provide, together, up to $10 billion over 10 years. Russia has agreed to contribute $2 billion of its own money. It has also agreed to adopt a set of guidelines that will allow it to receive assistance. Specifically it has agreed that it will provide for "effective monitoring, auditing, and transparency measures" and that it will "provide for adequate access for donor representatives at work sites." It has also agreed that the assistance will be free from taxes and other charges and that it will ensure

---

[126] "The most effective approach to reducing the risk is a multi-layered defense designed to block each step on the terrorist pathway to the a bomb. But securing nuclear weapons and materials at their source is the single most critical layer of this defense, where actions that can be taken now will do the most to reduce the risk of terrorist acquiring nuclear weapons and materials, at least cost." *Controlling Nuclear Warheads and Materials: A Report Card and Action Plan*, by Matthew Bunn et al. Project on Managing the Atom. March 2003.

[127] According to former Senator Sam Nunn, "some 20 tons of civilian HEU (highly enriched uranium) exists at 345 civilian research facilities in 58 countries, yet there are no international standards for securing these nuclear materials within a country." Sam Nunn, Co-Chairman of the Nuclear Threat Initiative. *Reducing the Threats from Weapons of Mass Destruction and Building a Global Coalition Against Catastrophic Terrorism*. Moscow, Russia. May 27, 2002.

---

adequate liability protections for donor countries and their personnel.[128] Each of these issues continued to hinder nonproliferation assistance to Russia, and all potential donors emphasized the need for their resolution before they provided additional assistance.

The G-8 leaders agreed that this program would initially focus on threat reduction and nonproliferation programs in Russia; they have since extended it to Ukraine. The United States considers its assistance to the other former Soviet states to be a part of its commitment under the Global Partnership. The United States would also like the Global Partnership to contribute to programs designed to redirect scientists in Iraq and Libya. During their 2004 meeting at Sea Island, Georgia, the participants agreed to consider this proposal. The participants have agreed that they could, individually, extend assistance to other nations, outside the specific Global Partnership, if these other nations adopt the Partnership's guidelines.

The G-8 leaders also invited other nations or organizations, such as the European Union, to contribute to the program. Norway and others in Europe have already outlined cooperative programs with Russia. At the G-8 summit in Evian, France, in 2003, six other nations in Europe (Sweden, Finland, Norway, Poland, Switzerland, and the Netherlands) joined the partnership. Seven additional nations (Australia, New Zealand, South Korea, Belgium, Denmark, Ireland, and the Czech Republic) joined during the 2004 summit in Sea Island, Georgia. President Bush, in a speech on February 11, 2004, specifically emphasized that the G-8 Global Partnership should expand its list of both donors and recipient nations.[129]

Some analysts have questioned how successful the Global Partnership will be in providing significant new funding for threat reduction and nonproliferation programs. The Partnership has received pledges for around $17 billion (including the $10 billion from the United States). Pledges of support received since Kananaskis may not necessarily extend into sustained funding over the next 10 years. As Senator Richard Lugar has noted, "many of our international partners will find it difficult to establish nonproliferation programs during a period of stagnating domestic economic growth."[130] However, as the annex to the 2009 Annual Report of the Global Partnership Working Group indicates, the participating nations continue to fund hundreds of projects in the recipient nations and expenditure continue to grow.[131]

Analysts initially questioned how the allies will set priorities and divide up responsibilities over different types of nonproliferation projects. In the statement released after the Kananaskis summit, they listed several projects, including the destruction of chemical weapons, dismantlement of decommissioned nuclear submarines, disposition of fissile materials, and employment of former weapons scientists as high-priority projects.[132] These areas remain a high priority in 2009. Most analysts agree that added funding would help to expand and accelerate each of these project areas. At the same time though, the Global Partnership does not rely on a

---

[128] "The G8 Global Partnership Against the Spread of Weapons and Materials of Mass Destruction." Statement by the Group of Eight Leaders. Kananaskis, Canada. June 27, 2002.

[129] The White House. "President announces New Measures to Counter the Threat of WMD." Fort Lesley J. McNair. February 11, 2004.

[130] Senator Richard Lugar has noted that "The G-8 initiative is not assured. "See Lugar, Richard G. "The Next Steps in U.S. Nonproliferation Policy." *Arms Control Today*. December 2002.

[131] G-8 Global Partnership, *2009 Report on the Global Partnership Working Group*, Annual Report, July 2009. http://www.canadainternational.gc.ca/g8/summit-sommet/2009/global_partnership-association_globale.aspx

[132] "The G8 Global Partnership Against the Spread of Weapons and Materials of Mass Destruction." Statement by the Group of Eight Leaders. Kananaskis, Canada. June 27, 2002.

---

single coordinating body to either identify new projects or set priorities among competing projects. Each nation allocates its own funds to those programs that it views as high-priority endeavors.

Extending CTR Beyond the Former Soviet Union

In the debate over the FY2003 Defense Authorization Bill, the Senate approved an amendment, proposed by Senator Richard Lugar, that would allow DOD to use up to $50 million in FY2003 CTR funds "outside the states of the former Soviet Union" to resolve "critical emerging proliferation threats and to take advantage of opportunities to achieve long-standing United States nonproliferation goals."[133] Senator Lugar argued that this type of effort could provide assistance to nations "seeking help in securing or destroying weapons or dangerous materials" and could also "create international standards of accountability for protecting and handling nuclear material and deadly pathogens." This legislation would also allow the United States to "undertake missions to secure dangerous materials or weapons that were at risk of falling into the wrong hands."[134]

The Senate and the Bush Administration supported Senator Lugar's proposal. The House, however, objected to this expansion of CTR, and the language was removed in conference. The Bush Administration requested a similar authorization in its Emergency Supplemental Appropriations Bill for FY2003. The Senate again approved the request and the House again rejected it; it was removed from the final version of the bill.

The Bush Administration again requested the authorization to spend up to $50 million in CTR funds outside the former Soviet Union in the FY2004 Defense Authorization Bill. The Senate again offered its unqualified support for this measure. The House, in contrast, argued that these types of programs would be better managed by the State Department than the Defense Department. It authorized the transfer of up to $78 million in CTR funds to the State Department Nonproliferation and Disarmament fund for use in threat reduction efforts outside the former Soviet Union. The conference committee, in its report on the FY2004 Defense Authorization Bill (P.L. 108-136), approved the President's request and permitted the use of up to $50 million in CTR funds outside the former Soviet Union. However, in deference to the House concerns, the committee language indicated that this funding could be used only for short-term projects; it also stated that the President should determine whether DOD was the agency that is most capable of implementing the planned project. The conferees stated that they would expect the President to assign the project to the most appropriate agency. The Bush Administration exercised this authority for the first time in mid-2004, when it provided assistance to Albania for the elimination of chemical weapons.[135]

In its version of the FY2006 Defense Authorization Bill, the Senate sought to alter the provision, so that the Secretary of Defense, rather than the President, could approve expenditures outside the former Soviet Union. The Senate argued that this change would streamline the procedure and make it easier for the United States to respond to sudden and emerging proliferation problems. The House, however, objected, and the conference committee did not accept the Senate provision.

---

[133] S. 2026, H.R. 4546, §1203.

[134] Lugar, Richard G. "The Next Steps in U.S. Nonproliferation Policy." *Arms Control Today*. December 2002.

[135] Warrick, Joby. Albania's Chemical Cache Raises Fears About Others. *Washington Post*. January 10, 2005. p. A1.

The 110th Congress addressed this issue again, both expanding the authority to spend CTR funds outside the former Soviet Union and to streamline the process of identifying and approving potential projects. As was noted above, Congress added $10 million to the CTR authorization to fund these programs, Further, it eliminated the requirement included in the FY2004 Authorization Act (P.L. 108-136) that limited the program to short-term projects that addressed sudden, emergency proliferation concerns. Instead, the conference report (P.L. 110-181, §1303), specifies that CTR programs outside the former Soviet Union are defined in a similar way to those inside the former Soviet Union. They would be programs designed to:

- Facilitate the elimination, and the safe and secure transportation and storage, of chemical or biological weapons, weapons components, weapons-related materials, and their delivery vehicles.

- Facilitate safe and secure transportation and storage of nuclear weapons, weapons components, and their delivery vehicles.

- Prevent the proliferation of nuclear and chemical weapons, weapons components, and weapons-related military technology and expertise.

- Prevent the proliferation of biological weapons, weapons components, and weapons-related military technology and expertise, which may include activities that facilitate detection and reporting of highly pathogenic diseases or other diseases that are associated with or that could be utilized as an early warning mechanism for disease outbreaks that could impact the Armed Forces of the United States or allies of the United States; and

- Expand military-to-military and defense contacts.

Congress emphasized its interest in expanding the CTR program beyond the borders of the former Soviet Union by noting, in Section 1306 of the FY2008 Defense Authorization Act, that CTR should be "strengthened and expanded, in part by developing new CTR initiatives." It stated that these new initiatives should "include broader international cooperation and partnerships, and increased international contributions." It also suggested that these new initiatives could include "programs and projects in Asia and the Middle East; and activities relating to the denuclearization of the Democratic People's Republic of Korea." Moreover, Congress mandated that the National Academy of Sciences conduct a study "to analyze options for strengthening and expanding the CTR Program."

The National Academy completed this study and released its report in April 2009. It recommended that the United States use a new, broader CTR program to engage nations around the world in a global effort to secure dangerous weapons and materials.[136] It also suggested that Congress authorize DOD to accept funds from other nations for use in CTR efforts. The FY2010 Defense Authorization Bill included this provision. Moreover, the Obama Administration has indicated that it supports efforts to expand CTR and DOE's nonproliferation assistance beyond the former Soviet Union; its budget request for FY2011 includes funds for this purpose in several program areas.

Those who support the expansion of CTR beyond the former Soviet Union argue that the United States could apply the model of threat reduction assistance that it has developed during the past

---

[136] National Academy of Sciences, *Global Security Engagement: A New Model for Cooperative Threat Reduction*, Washington, DC, April 2009.

18 years to help other nations secure and eliminate weapons or materials that might be attractive to terrorists. They point to nations such as Pakistan, where insecure nuclear materials might be at risk of theft or diversion by government officials or representatives of terrorist organizations.[137] Others, however, question whether a program like CTR can be applied successfully to nations outside the former Soviet Union. They note that these nations might not be willing to allow the United States access to facilities that house nuclear materials or weapons; that they might prefer to enhance, rather than reduce, the threat posed by their weapons of mass destruction; and that U.S. assistance in securing weapons might actually make it easier for the recipient nations to deploy and use the weapons. Some have also questioned whether the United States can legally provide assistance, under U.S. and international law, to nations that are not parties to the Nuclear Nonproliferation Treaty.[138]

Global Recognition of National Responsibility

One of the key themes in recent reviews of the proliferation threat and the potential link to terrorism is the recognition that nuclear, chemical, and biological materials reside in many nations around the world. Nations with research facilities for these materials often lack the basic accounting, security, export, and border control systems that the United States has spent more than 10 years trying to bring to Russia. Although few of these materials would be useful to those seeking to build nuclear weapons, they could be of use to those seeking a radiological dispersal device (dirty bomb) or a chemical or biological weapon. There is a growing consensus that the international community and individual nations should take steps to address problems with these materials, beyond those already in place under the International Atomic Energy Agency.[139]

The United States would not necessarily need to adopt new programs and appropriate new funds to address this problem. Some believe, as was noted above, that efforts to expand CTR programs beyond the former Soviet Union could help address the problem. But many believe that the IAEA, with the support of the United States, could take steps in this direction through its existing programs that help countries secure and account for radiological materials. The Chemical Weapons Convention also provides a mechanism that might help nations secure and account for chemical agents and materials. Consequently, at least initially, the effort to address this global problem could be more diplomatic and political than technical, with the United States and others using the "bully pulpit" to encourage other nations to recognize the problem and take steps within their own systems to address their own vulnerabilities.

In essence, this new global focus may serve to shape the second decade of U.S. threat reduction and nonproliferation assistance. During the first decade, the problem was dominated by concerns over the potential for the loss of control over nuclear materials and weapons in the former Soviet Union, and the solutions were dominated by U.S. programs to bring technical assistance to the former Soviet states. In the second decade, the problem is likely to be dominated by concerns

---

[137] See, for example, Gottemoeller, Rose and Rebecca Longsworth. *Enhancing Nuclear Security in the Counterterrorism Struggle: India and Pakistan as a New Region for Cooperation*. Carnegie Endowment for International Peace. Working Papers. Number 29. August 2002.

[138] See CRS Report RL31589, *Nuclear Threat Reduction Measures for India and Pakistan*, by Sharon Squassoni.

[139] Senator Sam Nunn, in outlining his proposal for a Global Coalition Against Catastrophic Terrorism, has stated that "our goal must be to see that all nations come under a system of international standards and inspection for the protection of dangerous nuclear materials." Remarks by Former U.S. Senator Sam Nunn, Chairman, Nuclear Threat Initiative. Carnegie Endowment for International Peace. International Nonproliferation Conference. November 14, 2002.

about the potential acquisition of nuclear, chemical, and biological materials by terrorist organizations. The solutions may be dominated by a growing sense of global cooperation in identifying and addressing weaknesses in a greater number of countries. U.S. funding and technical assistance may still play a dominant role, but other nations may also step in to offer their experience, expertise, and financial resources.

Author Contact Information

Amy F. Woolf
Specialist in Nuclear Weapons Policy
awoolf@crs.loc.gov, 7-2379